LIFTING THE VEIL

The World of Muslim Women

Phil & Julie Parshall

Authentic MEDIA

Copyright 2002 by Phil & Julie Parshall

09 08 07 06 05 04 7 6 5 4 3 2
Authentic Media
129 Mobilization Dr, Waynesboro, GA 30830, USA authenticusa@stl.org
and 9 Holdom Avenue, Bletchley, Milton Keynes, Bucks, MK1 1QR, UK

ISBN: 1-884543-67-7

Cover design by Paul Lewis
Cover photograph by Tom Richards

Printed in the United States of America

In Appreciation

Amma, Bhabi, and Meye—

Three Muslim women who graciously allowed us to peek beneath the veil.

Other Books by Phil Parshall

The Fortress and the Fire
New Paths in Muslim Evangelism
Bridges to Islam
Beyond the Mosque
The Cross and the Crescent
Inside the Community (Reprinted as Understanding
Muslim Teaching and Traditions.)
The Last Great Frontier
Divine Threads Within a Human Tapestry

Contents

Foreword By Dr. Miriam Adeney 9

Introduction 11

Chapter 1: Muhammad and Women 19

Chapter 2: Fundamentalism 37

Chapter 3: The Veil 55

Chapter 4: Modernity 71

Chapter 5: Heaven and Hell 87

Chapter 6: Folk Practices 101

Chapter 7: Circumcision 119

Chapter 8: Sex 131

Chapter 9: Marriage and Polygamy 149

Chapter 10: Married Women 169

Chapter 11: Mothers and Their Children 187

Chapter 12: Divorce 197

Chapter 13: Western Converts to Islam 211

Chapter 14: Witness and Conversion 225

Chapter 15: Discipleship 247

Chapter 16: The Path Ahead 265

Bibliography 269

Foreword

Before September 11, 2001, Muslims were important. Now the world knows it. This book helps us take a step toward understanding them.

Phil and Julie Parshall began their mission service in a Muslim community in Bangladesh. Here they settled down for twenty years, borrowing and lending cups of sugar; observing weddings, family quarrels, and funerals; having their own baby and finding baby-sitters from among their neighbors. Now Phil and Julie are ministering among 30,000 Muslims in a Manila slum.

In this book they have gathered insights gleaned from their many years of experience. We will glimpse Phil in Afghanistan, among the African Tuaregs, and attending a debate between Muslims at Yale University. Author of eight other books, seven on Islam, Phil here directs his attention to Muslim women. After all, as the Arab proverb says, "Women hold up half the sky." One tenth of the people in the world today are Muslim women.

The chapters brim with intriguing details. We learn about

the Prophet Muhammad's vigorous sex life. We learn that while the Sunnis view Muhammad's wife Aisha as the great love of his life, the Shiites view her as a jealous schemer. We learn reasons why some women want to wear veils today. A great richness of this book is the use of hadiths, authoritative traditional teachings, which are all well cited.

In these pages we see how fundamentalism can ooze over a society. "Less than a month after the *Shariah* Bill became law, the state-run Pakistan television began to censor its commercials. The first they whisked off the air was a tea bag ad that showed a man and a woman, both Islamically dressed, drinking tea together. That the couple are perhaps the best-known siblings in the country did not affect the decision. After much deliberation, the ad was allowed back on the air but only after a segment showing the couple smiling at each other and walking through a park together was cut. But a candy commercial was less fortunate. Its animated dancing jelly beans and sugar bears were permanently banished because dancing is un-Islamic" (Goodwin 1994:61).

Conversions among women do occur. The last three chapters of this book introduce us to Western women who have become Muslims, and moving in the opposite direction, Muslim women whose lives have been transformed by Jesus. In each case, their convictions are passionate, and their stories are heartfelt. Some suggestions for discipling have been included.

Phil and Julie themselves have seen a few of their Filipino Muslim women neighbors come into the kingdom of God through the Lord Jesus. In the end, it is Jesus' love for women and men that has compelled them to write this book.

Dr. Miriam Adeney
Author of *Daughters of Islam*

Introduction

Johura and Rumia—our first Muslim female buddies. It was March 1962. I was twenty-four, Julie was twenty-two, Johura was ten, and Rumia was eight. Julie and I had just arrived in the small village of Manikganj, East Pakistan (now Bangladesh). We had been married for a grand total of ten eventful months.

Our first look at this sleepy town with no electricity, running water, paved roads, or cars was somewhat shattering. But a more traumatic experience awaited us. Julie and I walked down a dusty road surrounded by taunting urchins. After all, I was the first white man to live in Manikganj since the creation of the world. We were a circus come to town.

There before us stood a dilapidated, holey tin house. This was to be our first home on the mission field. We had the misfortune of arriving at the hottest time of the year. With a tin roof and walls, our house was like an oven.

Among the gaping neighbors were Johura and Rumia, cute girls who lived with their mother and younger brother in a one-room shack just outside our bedroom window. Quickly they became our best friends. From our window, we observed Muslim life in its colorful mosaic of diversity. Marriage, birth, a funeral, squabbles, love, poverty, feasting, fasting, prayers, and a host of other social cycles took place both by sound and sight a few feet from our bedroom.

After three years in the village, our daughter Lyndi was born. With Johura and Rumia around, we were never in need of a babysitter. We had complete access to their home and they to ours. Borrowing of tea, sugar, and salt frequently took place through the bars on our bedroom window. This family introduced us to the culture of Muslim women. How grateful we are for their tutelage. They gracefully put up with all of our blunders and blabbering as we learned their language.

Later in our sojourn in Bangladesh, we met Amma, Bhabi, and Meye. These are sociological terms that refer to mother, sister-in-law, and daughter. This book is dedicated to the three of them. Our hearts were knit closely with these Muslim Bangladeshis. Being members of their extended family, we had access to their private lives. From them we learned the rituals of an upper-class, extremely religious Muslim family. Without their help, this book would be more theoretical than empirical. Our intimacy continues, though separated by several time zones, through letters, emails, and phone conversations.

As I have researched and written this book, I have had to struggle with two contradictory realities within the world of Muslim women.

The Negative

"A woman's heaven is under the feet of her husband."

"A man loves first his son, then his camel, and then his wife."

—Arab proverbs

Subjugation to men, for most Muslim women, is an accepted way of life. The male is a free agent with unquestionable authority. Women are to submit and dedicate their lives to making their husbands content. Education, however, can cause a Muslim woman to question such an unequivocal state of perpetual submission. An Iranian woman living in London writes of life in her homeland.

There is a place a mere five hours' flight from where I sit writing this book where I have a price, and that price is that of just half a man.

There is another world, a strange world where a man can kill me and escape execution unless my family pays to top up my worth to the price of a man.

If my father should die in this other world, I inherit one share to every two shares my brother gets. And if my husband dies I can expect only one-eighth of the life we built together.

There is a place, just five hours from here, where sons belong to their mother for only the first seven years of their lives.

There is a place where I am only half a witness in its courts.

There is a place where I need my father's permission to marry, no matter what my age.

> There is a place where I need my husband's consent to get a passport and his agreement before I can travel.
>
> There is a place, just five hours' flight from here, where I am but half a man. (Mosteshar 1996: preface)

Another writer explains the impact that fear has on Muslim women. She writes, "Through personal experience and close observation of others I have become certain that fear is the thing that most distorts women's characters. I was often living in a state of fear—lest I was discovered bleeding, writing a poem, choosing a husband. I even lived in fear of becoming pregnant with a girl rather than a boy" (Shaaban 1998:15).

A few days ago, I received an email from a close Bangladeshi friend who is a graduate of Princeton University. He writes, "I am looking into doing something to alleviate the sufferings of women and children. Women are still repressed, dowry killings go on, acid [is thrown] on women by rejected suitors, household servants are sexually abused and then thrown off apartment building roofs. Unbelievable things!"

The Positive

I have before me a letter written by our aforementioned Bangladeshi Muslim "daughter." She writes, "It is so wonderful to receive your mail. I could not check my tears because you are very much a part of our lives, a part of our family. We love you very, very much. I feel I am your other Lyndi. I miss you."

Love. Yes, Julie and I have been so privileged to see love, care, empathy, and sacrifice play out in the inner sanctums of Muslim families. The following pages will reveal terrible deprivations of women. But I have also sought to highlight the positive aspects of Muslim life for the female sex.

A professional woman from the United Arab Emirates who received her bachelor's and master of arts degree from a California university, reflects on her faith in the book *Price of Honor* by Jan Goodwin.

"My faith is important to me. I like being a Muslim, I enjoy the spiritual side of my life. Islam has given me a core of strength. If I hadn't had my faith I don't think I would have survived in the West. It helped me say no to drugs when everybody around me was using them, or putting me down because I refused to date. Today, it gives me peace. Islam is consistent and very structured, and because of this I believe it is an easier religion to follow than any other. Here everybody is fasting or praying at the same time. In the U.S., there are so many different religions, it must be very confusing" (Goodwin 1994:141).

A well-traveled Lebanese woman, Nadia Nouhid, adds her perspective.

"The Lebanese woman has no reason to envy any other woman in the world. I have lived in North and South America and have experienced different attitudes to women. I still like women to keep their pride, honour and dignity. We have beautiful traditions and should keep them. Cleanliness in body as well as in the mind is lovely. Women's honour is priceless; if she wins the whole world and loses her honour she won't be in an enviable position. The Western woman has lost her family. I love my family. I would not exchange my family happiness with anything, absolutely anything, in the world. I feel that the Western woman is lost. It is true that she enjoys more personal freedom then the Eastern woman and that she is more comfortable; she enjoys leisure and rest time—which we hardly have at all—but I feel we are still happier than Western women" (Mallouhi 1994:65–66).

Negative and positive. Work through the concepts, theological positions, and actual experiences of Muslim women as presented in this book. And then draw your own conclusions. Hopefully, at minimum, my writings will assist you in understanding the Muslim woman in a more loving and prayerful manner. This, along with prompting you to actively engage in witness to these "daughters of Ishmael," constitutes the focus and direction of *Lifting the Veil*. Sadly I am not able to provide answers to all of the issues raised in the following pages. But it is a start.

I have written in the first person throughout this book, but in reality this is a collaborative effort. Julie has been my guide, critic, and encourager. Therefore the authorship includes my beloved wife of over four decades. What a pure delight to have served our Lord together among Muslims for these many years. It is no exaggeration to say that, without Julie, my life's journey would never have been as productive, exciting, and fulfilling as it has been. And, for sure, I would not have authored nine books.

Lastly I would like to express my appreciation to my close friend, Dr. Ed Welch, who edited this book and to the many missionary women who responded to my questionnaire. Also I give my thanks to Dr. Miriam Adeney, noted scholar and author, for writing the foreword. SIM, a truly great mission, has so graciously given me freedom, encouragement, and stimulation. It has been a joy to be a member since 1989 when our original mission, International Christian Fellowship, and SIM merged.

All Quranic citations are from *The Meaning of the Glorious Koran*, translated by Mohammed Marmaduke Pickthall. This translation is highly regarded by Muslims worldwide.

I have quoted only the most authoritative *Al Bukhari Hadith* (Traditions). The form of citation I use for each Hadith is (9:10;83.6.17). Nine is the volume; 10 is the page number. The book is 83, the chapter is 6, and the number of the tradition is 17. This style of citation should enable the reader to find any Hadith, no matter which Al-Bukhari collection is used.

1

Muhammad and Women

J ulie and I were rummaging through a pile of used items near the back of a Pasadena, California, Salvation Army store when we heard the familiar sound of Bengali words wafting through the air. At that time, we had ministered in Bangladesh for sixteen years. We were on home assignment while I pursued doctoral studies at Fuller Seminary.

After looking around, we saw a handsome Bengali couple with a young child. Within minutes we were animatedly sharing life histories, as one is prone to do with gregarious Bengalis. Yusuf was working as an engineer with a multinational company based in Pasadena. He and his wife, Rani, were both from upper-class families in Bangladesh.

Very soon a warm friendship blossomed between us. We even took a three-day vacation together in San Francisco, staying with Yusuf's Muslim relatives. Rani was quite regular in her prayer time, while Yusuf was more secular and worldly. The opportunity arose on more than one occasion to share our faith with this delightful couple.

One evening we were in their apartment when other Muslim friends from Bangladesh joined us. There was a light atmosphere of cordiality and joking. Suddenly Yusuf said, "Muhammad must have had a powerful sex drive. Just think of having twelve sexual partners!" Then all the men laughed loudly. For the first time in my life, I had heard the Prophet Muhammad maligned by professing Muslims. In fact, it is the only time I have ever personally witnessed a Muslim making an off-color comment about the Apostle of Islam. In certain countries, this could warrant a prison sentence or, in Pakistan, even death.

According to all orthodox Muslim interpretations, Muhammad was exemplary in his dealing with the opposite sex. Data will be presented in this chapter that will seem to indicate otherwise. Muslim apologists will vociferously denounce any attempt to cast the Prophet in a negative light. That is understandable. But let the evidence presented stand or fall on its own merit. I can do no better than quote Islamic sources on the subject and allow judgments to be formed.

Muhammad the Emancipator

When studying history, it is important to remember that an event occurred in a specific manner. The problem that arises with history is not with the happening. Rather it is with items like the witnesses, recall, presuppositions, context, cultural considerations, documentation, and religious or political prejudices. Thus, the event can be, and often is, distorted by historians. Not that this process is intentional. Usually it is not. But fallibility abounds among secular and religious scribes the same as it has in decades and centuries past. When studying history, one needs to remember that an event occurred in a specific manner. All too often, little more than lip service is paid to this reality. Yes, we say others can be errant, but *we* have been preserved from error by accurate academia, or even better yet, by God Himself.

And now we come to the indisputable historical figure of the Prophet Muhammad. He was born, he got married, he gathered a significant following, and then he died. There are no dissenters to this set of facts. But controversies abound as we seek to fill in the details and interpretations of this man's sixty-two years in the desert of Arabia. Lest we as Christians be overly judgmental of the contradictions and enigmas that follow, may we be reminded of the myriads of interpretations that we have dogmatically asserted regarding the person of Jesus Christ!

Muslims begin the apologetic of their Prophet by highlighting the unbearable conditions that women supposedly endured in pre-Islamic Arabia. Mona Al Munajjed, author of *Women in Saudi Arabia Today*, writes about the relations between men and women during this time.

"At that time sexual permissiveness was the norm in Arabia, and men had the right to an unlimited number of women. For example a man could marry more than 10 wives at the same time. Conversely, cases of polyandry existed, where one woman was married to several men. A husband could have a mistress and the wife a lover without any restrictions. Both husbands and wives could exchange partners upon mutual agreement.

"Incest was practiced, with fathers marrying their daughters. A son was allowed to marry his stepmother after the death of his father. Prostitutes were recognizable by a flag on their tents, and men sought them whenever they liked. A man could divorce his wife just by saying the words of dismissal 'Go whenever you want', and she had no redress to law. A woman was an object to be inherited like money, but she could inherit nothing from her husband or her son" (Al Munajjed 1997:12–13).

While not affirming each of these items, my research does indicate that, overall, women were downtrodden and, in many instances, suffered deprivation. This, however, appears to be a reality within the majority of cultures throughout history. In our present, so-called, age of enlightenment, most religious spokespersons seem to put a spin on their treatment of women that portrays themselves as emancipators rather than victimizers. Therefore Muslims generally paint a grim picture of women in pre-Islamic times, thus allowing the contrast of pre- versus post-Islamic Arabia to overwhelmingly favor their benign treatment of women.

Bevan Jones, a long-term missionary to India, offers an alternative view of pre-Islamic women from the life of Muhammad's first wife.

"We might cite the case of the lot of married women in Mecca, where, as the result of contacts with superior civilizations, the laws in such matters were more liberal. It was here that Khadijah, the rich widow and trader, lived a life of comparative independence. It is certain that she owned real property, since she presented a house to her daughter, Zainab. Though she be viewed as an exceptional case, we know that the women of Mecca had shares in the sale and profits of merchandise conveyed by caravans, and from this we may assume that they held property" (Jones 1941:31).

In any event, Muhammad is extolled as the one who uplifts women and gives them unprecedented freedom. One of his most often quoted sayings is, "The best among you is he who is good to his family."

Muslim writer Syed Abul Hasan Ali Nadwi, in this soaring commendation, says, "If you study the life of the Prophet, peace be upon him, you will be struck by instances of his respect for the fair sex and his regard for sentiments which are not to be found in the lives of the greatest champions of the rights of women, nor in the lives of the most illustrious holy men and law-givers, and not in the lives of the other Apostles. The pains the Blessed Prophet took to please his wives and make them happy, his sharing in their legitimate recreational activities, his careful impartial justice to them—these were of surpassing charm and nobleness" (Nadwi 1983:170). To the outsider, these words have a ring of hyperbole. But it is important to try to enter into the heart of the devotee. Though not correct, as per orthodox Islam, multitudes of Muslims regard Muhammad as a sinless example of manhood. He could do no wrong. The Prophet is the exemplar par excellence. His attitudes, words, and deeds are to be maximally emulated. A Muslim is mentally and spiritually programmed to extol rather than critique Muhammad.

Interestingly the Prophet finds defenders even among Western feminist academicians such as retired Harvard professor, Annemarie Schimmel.

"It would be astonishing indeed if Islam were a religion outspokenly inimical toward women, for it was the Prophet Muhammad himself who said in one of his most quoted statements: 'God has made dear to me from your world women and fragrance, and the joy of my eyes is in prayer.' Women smell nice; "good" (tayyib) and "fragrance" (tib) both come from the same Arabic root. We should also remember that the Prophet's first wife, Khadija, with whom he lived in monogamous union for twenty-five years, supported and comforted him throughout the unprecedented spiritual shock brought about by the initial revelations" (Schimmel 1997:21).

No one would dispute Muhammad was a lover of women. It is also not surprising that he found them to smell nice. But all of that seems like a weak argument in regard to how he treated or regarded women. Schimmel appears to have a blind spot in her mostly unconditional praise of the Prophet. She has authored a number of books on Islam, but she seems to have put aside the usually critical Harvard faculties when it comes to interacting with the negative aspects of the world's second most adhered to religion.

In the Traditions, Muhammad is often set forth as being extremely careful in his dealings with the opposite sex. M.I. Siddiqi wrote about this in *Rights of Allah and Human Rights.* "Touching of women is also forbidden, except in cases of grave emergency endangering life or health. A Tradition says: 'If a person touches a woman with whom he has no legitimate relations, his hands will be burnt on the Day of Judgment.' Whenever a woman or a party of women came to the Prophet for taking the pledge of Islam, he refused to stretch his hands. Once Umaymah bint Ruqayqah came with a few women to take the pledge and asked the Prophet to give his hand. The Prophet refused saying: 'I do not shake hands with women; verbal declaration is enough for them'" (Siddiqi 1981:87–88).

Throughout the Muslim world, women generally salute, nod, or smile when they are greeting the opposite sex. They are simply following the example of the Prophet. In one instance, a foreign young man put out his hand to steady an unknown Muslim woman who was about to fall. Her nearby husband went into a rage and threatened to assault the foreigner for his immoral act.

While visiting Egypt, I was personally offended by the Muslim shopkeepers who sought to shake hands with my wife. I knew they would never allow me to touch their wives. They were simply enjoying freedom with the tourists, most of whom thought nothing of their gesture. I guess I have lived in the cocoon of Islamic culture too long!

The Prophet and His Wives

Muhammad, under direct revelation from Allah, was permitted to marry an unlimited number of wives. The Quran also makes it clear that female captives taken in war could be appropriated by him as his concubines. It says, "O Prophet! Lo! We have made lawful unto thee thy wives unto whom thou hast paid their dowries, and those whom thy right hand possesseth of those whom Allah hath given thee as spoils of war" (Quran 33:50).

As will be seen in the ensuing chapters, this privilege was given exclusively to Muhammad. His followers were to marry a maximum of four wives at a time. This is dependent on the husband's ability to financially care for the wives. A further demand was that all spouses be treated with absolute equality. This latter command is viewed by many, Muslim and non-Muslims alike, to be an impossible restriction. Thus we find the vast majority of Muslim marriages to be monogamous. Muhammad, however, was the exception to any ceiling regarding the number of wives or concubines.

It is interesting to note how earthy the Quran is as it deals with such topics. Muhammad is allowed to give these instructions to his wives with the imprimatur of ultimate authority. As in most of the Quran, Allah is doing the speaking:

"O Prophet! Say unto thy wives: If ye desire the world's life and its adornment, come! I will content you and will release you with a fair release. But if he desire Allah and His messenger and the abode of the Hereafter, then lo! Allah hath prepared for the good among you an immense reward....

"Whosoever of you is submissive unto Allah and His

messenger and doeth right, We shall give her reward twice over....O ye wives of the Prophet! Ye are not like any other women. If ye keep your duty (to Allah), then be not soft of speech, lest he in whose heart is a disease aspire (to you), but utter customary speech. And stay in your houses....Obey Allah and His messenger" (Quran 33:28–33).

The wives of Muhammad were expected to be exemplary in behavior. They were to shun worldliness and experience repose in Muhammad and the promise of eternal life. Submission to Allah and Muhammad were the imperatives of life. Speech should be circumspect so that no man would be tempted to seduce a wife of the Prophet. Confinement to the home would further guarantee the moral purity of the wives.

Contemporary Muslim women are taught from childhood to focus on the positive attributes of these saintly women. They are to make moral and ethical decisions based on Quranic and Hadith teachings, which were given to Muhammad's wives. This is safe territory for the devout female who earnestly desires to please Allah.

There is no record regarding how many women Muhammad had physical relations with. The number of official wives is usually set at twelve. Slaves, captives, and concubines represent another category, which is numerically impossible to document. Authoritative Hadith, however, do point to Muhammad having a relaxed and informal relationship with these women. One Hadith says, "Any of the female slaves of Medina could take hold of the hand of Allah's Apostle and take him wherever she wished" (8:62; 72.61.97).

This Tradition doesn't seem to be in sync with the ultra conservative understanding of modesty between Muslim women and men. In almost all Islamic countries, it is strictly forbidden for men and women to touch in public, even if married to each other. In Saudi Arabia such behavior would likely lead to arrest and imprisonment. So much for following the example of the Prophet!

Men particularly enjoy focusing on the sexual prowess of Muhammad. This Hadith illustrates the point rather colorfully.

"Anas bin Malik said The Prophet used to visit all his wives in a round, during the day and night and they were eleven in number. I asked Anas, 'Had the Prophet the strength for it?' Anas replied, 'We used to say that the Prophet was given the strength of thirty (men)'" (1:165; 5.13.268).

A point needs to be made here concerning Islam and sexuality. One could form an opinion that Muslims have a Victorian view of sex. After all, look at the full-body veils that many women are coerced to wear. Behavior such as adultery and fornication are punishable by death. But in reality, sex is a frequent topic of conversation, but these conversations are almost always either just among men or just among women.

Also the lines are clearly drawn. Islam teaches that legitimate sex is to be enjoyed and celebrated only within marriage. Slave girls and concubines are almost non-existent in current times. Therefore, the Prophet is regarded with a measure of envy when Anas declares him to have the sexual strength of thirty men. It is not considered immoral for Muhammad to have had frequent sex with his multiple wives.

Muslims strongly assert that the Prophet, in later life, married only widows and women with whom political alliances could be formed. They point out his strong monogamous marriage to Khadija that lasted for over twenty-five happy years. It was only after her death that Muhammad began taking multiple wives. Muslims passionately refute the charge that the Prophet ended his last decade on earth as a lustful, dirty old man. While not affirming this proposition, truth probably lies somewhere between a focus on politics and sexual enjoyment. Muhammad definitely had a focus on the physical.

This Islamic Tradition allows us to see the Prophet's fixation through the marital advice he gave to a friend.

"[The Prophet] then asked me, 'Have you got married?' I replied in the affirmative. He asked, 'A virgin or a matron?' I replied, 'I married a matron.' The Prophet said, 'Why have you not married a virgin, so that you may play with her and she may play with you?' Jabir replied, 'I have sisters (young in age) so, I liked to marry a matron who could collect them all and comb their hair and look after them'" (3:176; 34.35.310).

In *The Cross and the Crescent*, I documented a rather startling Hadith, which I have included along with my comments.

"Allah's Apostle used to visit Um Haram bint Milhan and she was the wife of Ubada bin As-Samit. One day the Prophet visited her and she provided him with food and started looking for lice in his head. Then Allah's Apostle slept...[Translator's note: The Prophet was very clean as he used to take a bath daily. It is not logical that he could have had lice in his head. Searching for lice does not necessarily mean that there were any.] (9:108; 87.12.130).

"A number of questions arise in regard to the Prophet's behavior as set forth in this Hadith. Why did Muhammad repeatedly visit this married lady? There is no indication he went to see her husband, whose name is given only incidentally. The relationship was close enough that the woman fed the Prophet. Intimacy then proceeds to the point where the lady is recorded searching through the Prophet's hair in pursuit of any lice which may have taken up residence, during which time he falls asleep. This familiarity seems to exceed the boundaries of decorum set by Muhammad himself.

"The note at the conclusion of this Tradition is not focused on the propriety of the Prophet's actions. Rather it digresses into a defense of Muhammad's bathing habits and subsequent cleanness of body, which would disallow the possibility of lice being found in his hair. I am not too surprised at this shift of emphasis. Muslims are often so taken up with the minutia of ritual that they miss some of the larger issues of life" (Parshall 1994:168–169).

Aisha

This brings us to the most famous of the marriages of Muhammad. First, we must look at the indisputable age of his bride: "Narrated Aisha that the Prophet married her when she was six years old and he consummated his marriage when she was nine years old, and then she remained with him for nine years (i.e., till his death)" (7:50; 62.39.64).

Even though Muslims regard this marriage as a political expediency uniting two families in the cause of Islam, it is obvious that Aisha was more than a pragmatic necessity to the Prophet. He was madly in love with her to the point that almost all Muslims concur that Aisha was his favorite wife (after his first wife, Khadija). This, in itself, is a contradiction. Muslims, according to the Quran, are not allowed to show favoritism to any one wife.

Child marriage was common in seventh-century Arabia. This early commitment solidified the relationship with the view that the physical consummation of the marriage took place after the wife's first menstrual period. Some critics have doubted that Aisha could have had her period as early as nine years of age, but this, however, is not impossible. That notwithstanding, it is fair to question the propriety of a fifty-three-year-old man having sex with a girl of nine. To Muslims, this was the will of Allah, and it is not to be an issue of any consideration.

There is a difference of opinion between Sunnis and Shiites regarding Aisha as documented by Geraldine Brooks in her excellent book, *Nine Parts of Desire*.

"Today, if you ask Sunni Muslims about Aisha, they will tell you she was the great love of Muhammad's later life, a formidable teacher of Islam, a heroine in battle. But ask Shiites, and they will describe a jealous schemer who destroyed the prophet's domestic peace, plotted against his daughter Fatima, spied on the household and fomented a tragic factional bloodletting that left the Muslim nation permanently divided.

"Aisha—Arabic for "life"—is one of the most popular girls' names in the Sunni Muslim world. But among Shiites it is a term of exasperation and abuse. When a Shiite girl misbehaves, her mother is likely to upbraid her with a shout of 'You Aisha!'" (Brooks 1995:77–78).

Since Sunnis constitute ninety percent of the world's Islamic population, the positive view of Aisha dominates. Yet it must be stated that the Traditions do point out that Aisha should not exactly be conferred with sainthood.

Her jealousy of Muhammad's other wives was a documented reality. Geraldine Brooks comments on this.

"In the year or two after Aisha moved in, Muhammad married three more women, all war widows: Hafsah, the twenty-year-old daughter of his close friend Omar; an older woman, Zeinab, whose generosity had earned her the name "Mother of the Poor," and who died just eight months later; and Umm Salamah, a famous beauty whose arrival caused Aisha the first pangs of the jealousy that would blight the rest of her life. When Aisha learned about the marriage to Umm Salamah, 'I was exceedingly sad,' she said, 'having heard much of her beauty.' She called on the new wife and found her 'twice as beautiful and graceful as she was reputed to be'" (Brooks 1995:79).

Throughout the Traditions, one finds repeated references to Aisha's desire to have a singular relationship with the Prophet. Sharing her husband with other young and beautiful wives brought unmitigated sorrow to teenaged Aisha. Quarrels frequently broke out among these wives. Aisha herself authored a Hadith that reveals her feisty nature: "Narrated Aisha: The things which annul the prayers were mentioned before me. They said, 'Prayer is annulled by a dog, a donkey and a woman (if they pass in front of the praying people).' I said, 'You have made us (i.e. women) dogs'" (1:291; 9.13.490).

Was Aisha the original Muslim feminist? She pondered as to the reason a woman was categorized with such animals as dogs and donkeys. It is unfortunate that women gained entrance into this list of prayer-nullifying objects. But the chauvinistic male would respond by pointing out the overpowering physical distraction of the female form comes into competition with a faith encounter with the unseen God of the universe.

Through a simple process of deduction, Aisha concluded that her worth was but that of a dog. And it must be pointed out that dogs in Middle Eastern culture are animals of filth. They are not seen as the cuddly, shampooed, pampered animals that are kept as house pets in contemporary Western society.

Another indication of Aisha's aggressive temperament is startlingly revealed in this encounter she had with Muhammad. She has recorded it in the Hadith:

> Narrated Aisha: I used to look down upon those ladies who had given themselves to Allah's Apostle and I used to say, "Can a lady give herself (to a man)?" But when Allah revealed:
>
> > You (O Muhammad) can postpone (the turn of) whom you will of them (your wives) and you may receive any of them whom you will; and there is no blame on you if you invite one whose turn you have set aside (temporarily). (Quran 33:51)
>
> I said to the Prophet, "I feel that your Lord hastens in fulfilling your wishes and desires" (6:295; 60.240.311).

This, indeed, is a low view of Allah transmitting His divine will to mankind. Aisha is obviously upset that Muhammad is given complete freedom to choose when and how frequently he will spend the night with which wife. In other Hadith, the wives' displeasure over this practice is amplified. But then comes this heavenly revelation. This word should cause all complaints to immediately cease. Allah's will has been revealed.

But Aisha cannot help but comment adversely on the fact that Quranic revelation seems to reinforce Muhammad's personal "wishes and desires." She is irritated that she is forced to share her beloved husband with multiple wives. So she criticizes how Allah interacts with His anointed and chosen Prophet. One can only speculate as to how Muhammad responded to his teenaged, favorite wife. Most likely it would be to affirm the sovereign will of Allah! Muslim theologians have consistently affirmed that Muhammad is a completely passive instrument in the process of scripture transmission. His "wishes and desires" are supposedly irrelevant as to what ends up being the inerrant, indisputable word of God.

I have heard many Muslims forcefully deny that the Quran deals with the mundane. They long to interpret Allah's word as high and exalted. The above is but one of many illustrations of how the Quran interacts with highly personal issues in the life of the Prophet.

Aisha was the wife who generated the most jealousy among the spouses. Brooks addressed this in *Nine Parts of Desire*.

"Despite his attempts at fairness, the whole community seems to have become aware that Aisha was his favorite wife. Muslims who wanted to send him a gift of food began timing their presents for the days they knew he would be spending in Aisha's apartment. Since Muhammad lived so humbly, these gifts often provided his household's only luxuries. Umm Salamah, for one, bitterly resented the preference shown to Aisha. 'I see that the rest of us are as nothing,' she said when yet another basket of goodies arrived on Aisha's day. Enraged, she flounced off to complain to Fatima, Muhammad's daughter" (Brooks 1995:81).

One concludes that there was a high level of disunity and intrigue among the wives of the Prophet. Comparisons of beauty were common, but the central issue related to how often Muhammad slept with each of his wives. In that, the Prophet's freedom had the very imprimatur of Allah.

Aisha was but a teenager when Muhammad died. Because of her close relationship with the Prophet, she became an authoritative figure within Islam. Some 2,210 Hadith were originally attributed to her. However, ninth-century scholars, in their bias against women, authenticated only 174 of them (Brooks 1995:87).

Aisha lived another fifty years after Muhammad died. She derived her considerable influence from two sources: (1) Her status as the favorite wife of the Prophet, and (2) the fact that her father was Abu Bakr, the successor to Muhammad. In the minds and hearts of millions of Muslim women, Aisha lives on as a fantasy figure of a beautiful young girl who was the lover of the greatest man who has ever lived. It is as if Aisha never grew old, somewhat akin to the American perception of the ever-youthful John F. Kennedy.

Zainab

By far the most controversial marriage of the Prophet was to Zainab, his cousin. Muhammad arranged the marriage of Zainab to Zeyd, his adopted son. From all indications they had a happy relationship.

One morning Muhammad went to Zeyd's home. Zainab spoke to the Prophet and invited him in, explaining that her husband was not at home. The Hadith indicates that Muhammad was suddenly stricken with a passionate desire for Zainab and quickly left the home.

When Zeyd returned, Zainab explained Muhammad's actions. It became clear to both husband and wife that the

Prophet desired to marry Zainab. Zeyd went to Muhammad with his proposal to divorce Zainab so that the Prophet could marry her.

Muhammad was hesitant to marry the divorced wife of his adopted son. But while pondering this dilemma, Muhammad received the following word from Allah, a word that has now been enshrined as holy scripture in the Quran: "So when Zeyd had performed the necessary formality (of divorce) from her, We gave her unto thee in marriage, so that (henceforth) there may be no sin for believers in respect of wives of their adopted sons, when the latter have performed the necessary formality (of release) from them. The commandment of Allah must be fulfilled. There is no reproach for the Prophet in that which Allah maketh his due" (Quran 33:37,38).

With this authentication for the divorce, Zeyd proceeded to free Zainab to marry Muhammad. No reproach for the Prophet. But, how do Muslims feel about this scenario? Actually, the ones I have talked to are considerably embarrassed. It is the marrying of an adopted son's former wife that presents the problem. Does this not come close to incest? Overall, Muslims just prefer not to talk about it. Also, they are very hesitant to adopt children. The whole episode, it seems, is preferably forgotten.

As this chapter concludes, I think it is best to let the reader render his or her own judgment on Muhammad and his dealing with women in general and his wives in particular. Muslims see no real problem. All of Muhammad's actions were within the allowable will of Allah. The non-Muslim will likely have reservations. And so the controversy continues. Some of the issues raised in this chapter have an important influence on Muslim attitudes toward women, as will be seen throughout the remainder of this book.

2

Fundamentalism

Just a few floors below the well-known library at Yale Law School, where Bill and Hillary Clinton met, is a commodious yet somewhat austere classroom. Terraced steps lead to theater-like, curved rows of several hundred unattractive student chairs, which seem like a more appropriate setting for a tenth grade English class than a training ground for future presidents.

This was the venue for a rather rancorous two-day symposium between liberal (modern) and fundamentalist (orthodox) Muslim intellectuals. During the fall of 1993, I was a research fellow at Yale and thus had the privilege of attending this unique encounter between Muslims of varying theological convictions. Opinions were dogmatically asserted.

At times I wondered if I might be a front-row observer to the first jihad to occur within the hallowed halls of Yale Law School. At the end, I congratulated one of the liberal scholars for holding his ground during volatile attacks on his position. He slowly drew his index finger from left to right across his neck and said, "Yes, but will I survive?"

One of the issues that drew the most heat was the suggestion that the Quranic allowance for beating a rebellious wife should be reevaluated in light of modern-day cultural norms. With one angry voice, the fundamentalists accused the liberals of being more concerned about academic reputation than with maintaining fidelity to Allah's Word, which is unchanging, inerrant, and relevant for all ages and contexts. The few women in the room remained stoically mute throughout the debate.

Muslim fundamentalists are becoming more vocal and aggressive. Liberals, although still a small minority, are carefully tiptoeing onto largely uncharted turf. Their discordant, yet bold, voice is being courageously raised in protest to the status quo where tradition rules the day. Increasingly, the battle rages over the status of women.

A widely recognized Islamic academician, Seyyed Nasr, presents the traditional view of Muslim women.

"Although both the male and the female are assigned different roles by nature, in Islam the roles of men and women are seen as complementary rather than competitive. As human souls, both the male and the female are absolutely equal in their relationship with their Creator; and as Muslims both the male and the female need to cultivate the same virtues and perform the same Islamic rites, and before God they bear the same accountability for their actions.

"Islamic rites and rituals are basically the same for both men and women. Performance of the rites may differ in minor details for women because of their different role; for example, the woman may not join the congregational Friday prayers held in the mosque but can perform the prayer at home. She may not join the funeral procession, and she is not supposed to take part in the burial rites. She is also exempted from saying the five prayers during menstruation and childbirth. The reasons for her exemptions are obvious. Islam is known as *Din al-fitrah* (a way of life according to the nature of the male and female) and *Din al-sahl* (a way of life in which there is ease). As such, the performance of the religious rites and ceremonies is based on the consideration of offering ease to the performer, which enables women to perform their own role efficiently" (Nasr 1987:212).

Dr. Jamal A. Badawi, head of a Muslim college in London, serves on the High Council of Islamic Affairs, the highest authority that makes decisions on issues relating to Muslim faith and doctrine. He was formerly on the faculty of Al Azhar University in Cairo. With credentials such as these, his searing critique of the fundamentalists is surprising.

In Jan Goodwin's book, *Price of Honor,* she records Badawi as saying, "Very few Muslim countries have given women their full rights, and both Islamic law and the message of Islam have been violated. But today, petro-Islam with its vast amounts of money is letting loose on the Islamic world a wave of fundamentalism. The movement, largely funded by the Saudis and Kuwaitis, is pushing a doctrine that is anti-woman, anti-intellectual, anti-progress, and anti-science" (Goodwin 1994:6).

Badawi has ventured into areas where few reputed Islamic theologians dare trespass. The place of Muslim women is considered by the orthodox to be a watershed issue. One need only look at Afghanistan, Saudi Arabia, and Iran to observe how inextricably linked women are to fundamentalism. Traditionalists believe the Quran, Hadith, and Islamic history are all at stake. If women are allowed equal rights with men, the very fabric of Islam will be threatened.

Interestingly, Christianity has bypassed certain passages of the Bible by reading them in a cultural and time-bound context. Few church-attending women wear a head covering while worshiping, keep silent in church, or avoid wearing pretentious jewelry. Islam, much more so than Christianity, embraces hermeneutical literalism. For many Muslims, the badge of fidelity to their faith is overtly measured by how their women are conforming to the outward restrictions imposed by the "guardians of the Faith."

Fundamentalism Illustrated

There are those who designate Pakistan as the most ideal Muslim nation in the world. Censors in that country are kept busy in their efforts to ensure that the purity of Islam is maintained. Jan Goodwin, a widely-traveled author, highlights some of the humorous extremes of these "defenders of the faith."

"Less than a month after the *Shariah* Bill became law, the state-run Pakistan television began to censor its commercials. The first they whisked off the air was a tea bag ad that showed a man and a woman both Islamically dressed, drinking tea together. That the couple are perhaps the best-known siblings in the country did not affect the decision. After much deliberation, the ad was allowed back on the air but only after a segment showing the couple smiling at each other and walking through a park together was cut. But a candy commercial was less fortunate. Its animated dancing jelly beans and sugar bears were permanently banished because dancing is un-Islamic" (Goodwin 1994:61).

Few outsiders have ever heard of a Muslim practice in which girls are given in marriage to the Quran, but it is a reality in the Sind province of Pakistan. Ibn Warraq has authored a searing critique of Islam in his book, *Why I am Not A Muslim*. In it he documents this unique ceremony:

"Forced seclusion sometimes takes a bizarre and tragic form, as in the case of those Muslim girls known as the Brides of the Koran, who are compelled by their families to marry the Koran. In large feudal, land-owning families, especially in the province of Sind, women are allowed to marry only within the family—in many cases only to first cousins—to ensure that the family property stays in the family.... When the family runs out of eligible male cousins, the young woman is forced to marry the Koran in a ceremony exactly like a real wedding except that the bridegroom is lacking. The bride is sumptuously dressed, guests are invited, food, and festivities follow. At the ceremony itself, the bride is instructed to place her hand on the Koran, and she is wedded to the holy book. The rest of her life is spent in total seclusion from the outside world. She is not allowed to see a man—in some cases, not even on television. These brides are expected to devote their time to studying the Koran or doing craftwork. Such desolate emptiness takes its toll, and many of the brides of the Koran become mentally ill. As one out of an estimated 3,000 brides of the Koran in the Sind put it, 'I wish I had been born when the Arabs buried their daughters alive. Even that would have been better than this torture'" (Warraq 1995:326).

Bizarre indeed! However, some may protest, and point to Catholic nuns who may be part of a cloistered order and consider themselves to be brides of Christ. The operative word that highlights the difference between these groups is "forced." Nuns make their choice voluntarily, apart from family compulsion. At any time, they are free to exit their order. This is not true of the "Brides of the Koran." Familial and societal pressure seals their destiny.

While in India on a speaking engagement, I picked up a local newspaper with a front-page article that pungently

41

described the sad plight of young Muslims girls. It said that teenage girls would be required to wear the burqa outside of their homes in Kanapur. They were also forbidden from wearing lipstick to college, a practice that is seen as too provocative.

India is not an Islamic nation under Shariah law. Rather it has a Hindu majority, with an approximate twelve percent Muslim population. Pockets of Muslims cluster in certain areas of the country, allowing fundamentalists the opportunity to impose their brand of Islam in these localities.

In the Philippines, I witnessed a rather confined squatter community of 30,000 Muslims. A large sign at the entrance to the neighborhood says that all females who enter must cover their head with some type of cloth. It is amusing to watch the girls take off their coverings as soon as they exit the gate. In another Muslim area of Manila, a signboard assures the "daughters of Ishmael" that they will burn in hell forever if they do not keep their heads covered at all times while outside their homes.

In an Islamic city on Mindanao, an island in the Southern Philippines, there is a huge billboard that shows the pictures of two girls. One is a young lady with a modest dress and head covering. Underneath is the word *halal* (permitted). The other girl is wearing a T-shirt and jeans with nothing on her head. Splashed across her picture is the word *haram* (prohibited).

These messages have a profound effect on the psychology of the women growing up in these cultures. In her book on Muslim women in India, Anees Jung wrote about an Indian Muslim woman who pensively reflects on the condition of her mother's maid.

"When Kulsoom Bi opens the door I recognize the look— gentle, withdrawn, guarded. She has worked in my mother's house and I have watched her for long hours cooking, cleaning, going to the bazaar, her head always draped. She even goes to sleep with her head draped. In the year I have known her I have never seen her hair. Nor have I known what she is all about. The bits that I know of her life, her early marriage, her unemployed husband, her insane daughter and her *jhuggi* that gets washed away every other monsoon—do not explain her look, her immense silence, one which I have taken for granted. For it is also the silence of my mother" (Jung 1993:ix).

Attitudes influenced by fundamentalist thinking cause confusion and anger in a Muslim Algerian home. Bouthaina Shaaban, author of *Both Right and Left Handed—Arab Women Talk About Their Lives,* talked to one woman about this.

"'There is no hope for women,' Farida burst out. 'We are going backwards, not forwards. In my day we could invite our boyfriends home for tea or to play a record but now, particularly after the appearance of this Muslim Brotherhood, my brother won't even allow my sister to speak to a boy. How can things ever improve if the teacher at my son's school tells the children that God doesn't like women driving cars, smoking cigarettes or putting on make-up? So my son, who is only six years old, comes out of school demanding to go home with his friend because it is his friend's father who is driving the car and doesn't want to come with me because I am driving and I am a *woman*. Once home he says, "Mum, why do you smoke if God has asked you not to smoke? Why do you put on make-up if our religion disapproves of it?" How can my child's generation move forward on the woman question? Even to talk about contraceptives—let alone use them—is a sin according to men. Women should breed continuously to prove they are having good relationships with their husbands'" (Shaaban 1988:184).

Punishment

Is it not true that most any set of postulates can be proven anecdotally? This is part of the danger of this section. Fundamentalist Islam has provided a theological and pragmatic interpretative framework for potential violations against the female sex. In this section, I deal particularly with this reality. The illustrations cited are not applicable throughout the entire Muslim world. But unfortunately, they are common enough to be frequently cited by the media.

A BBC commentator made the dogmatic assertion that one-third of all women in the world have been victims of some sort of physical abuse by men. While granting that this estimate is speculative, we are still faced with the reality of millions of battered women. Why this? Is it because of men's aggressive nature or perhaps their physical prowess? Are women easy to take advantage of because of their smaller stature and, often to be found, gentle dispositions? Or are they just victims of perpetuated history? The idea is that this is the way it has always been and always will be. Submission to the inevitable becomes the norm.

If this is a universal phenomenon, why pick on Islam? Jewish men pray a prayer that thanks God they were not born a woman. For centuries a Hindu widow was expected to throw herself onto the raging flames of her husband's funeral pyre. While visiting the Dalai Lama's palace in Lhasa, I observed shabbily dressed Tibetan women bow prostrate before images of Buddha and then place money in the nearby containers. It seemed these offerings could have better been directed toward their own pressing needs. Feminists in the West have long taken issue with Paul's bias toward male supremacy in his New Testament writings. Ephesians five has been the subject of strained exegesis where Paul plainly exhorts wives to submit to their husbands in all things.

But, to me at least, all of the above is a different issue than the clear allowance, as mentioned earlier, for the Muslim husband to beat his wife if she persists in some sort of rebellious behavior (Quran 4:34). This license, given directly from Allah, has been invoked innumerable times by husbands who feel they have somehow been harassed by an unsubmissive wife. There is no judge, no jury, and no 911 to call. Allah has spoken.

It is on this theological framework and its extrapolation that fundamentalists have felt justified to coerce women to conform to the way they think female followers of the Prophet should behave. The extreme punishments that are meted out to the so-called erring are shocking. In order to avoid charges of sensationalism, I have limited myself to a few documented citations of this widespread reality.

Malaysia, a Muslim country with a significant Chinese population, seems to be moving toward extremism, as indicated by an occurrence near the capital city, Kuala Lumpur. This is an excerpt from *Asiaweek* magazine.

"For three young Malaysian women last month, Friday the 13th lived up to its reputation as a dark day. The unlucky trio took part in the Miss Malaysia Petite pageant at a hotel in Selangor state, just outside Kuala Lumpur. The show went smoothly, watched by an enthusiastic, multiracial audience of men and women. The young ladies paraded in sporting outfits, swimsuits (discreetly covered by scarves) and long evening gowns then waited nervously for the results. Fahyu Hanim and Noni Mohamad beamed upon hearing they had won first and second runner-up prizes. But, as the excited teenagers congratulated each other, they were suddenly surrounded by stern-faced officials from Selangor's Islamic Affairs Department.

"Fahyu, Noni and colleague Sharina Shaari—all ethnic Malays—were told they had contravened Islamic regulations. As stunned guests watched in disbelief, the tearful girls— their shimmering gowns draped with their winners' sashes and their arms toting their trophies—were dragged out of the ballroom and bundled into a jeep. It took them to a nearby police station where the trio became the first Malaysians to be charged with indecent exposure for taking part in a beauty contest. Two weeks later they were found guilty and fined 400 ringgit (about $160) each. On Aug. 1, they will face a second charge of contravening a Selangor state *fatwa* [Islamic decree] prohibiting Muslim women from taking part in such pageants. If found guilty, they can be again fined as well as jailed. The state prosecutor has urged the court to impose a stiff sentence as a warning to other Muslim women" (Mitton 1997:22).

Iran has a religious police force that is one of the most oppressive in the world. Betty Mahmoody, writer of the bestseller, *Not Without My Daughter,* based on her experience in Iran, documents some of the excesses of the police force.

> As we stepped into the street, the Pakon (religious police) pulled forward quickly, screeching to a halt in front of us. Four lady pasdar jumped out and surrounded us. One of them did all the talking.
> "You are not Iranian?" she asked accusingly in Farsi.

"No."

"Where are you from?"

"I am from America," I said in Farsi.
She spoke sharply and rapidly into my face,
sorely testing my limited knowledge of the
language....
"Tell her that I can understand a few words,
nothing else."
This mollified the lady pasdar somewhat, but
she jabbered on further until Mahtob
explained, "She stopped you because your
socks have wrinkles in them."
I pulled up my offensive socks and the lady
pasdar turned to go, leaving Mahtob with the
final directive, "Tell your mother, do not ever
go out on the street again with wrinkly socks."
(Mahmoody 1987:260)

Goodwin documented a practice that causes one to cringe
with vicarious pain.

"Faribah insisted that the authorities had become so
violent that the Revolutionary Guards drive around the city
in motorbike gangs removing lipstick from women with razor
blades. I was sure the tale must be apocryphal until I learned
later that Iran's interior minister had given an interview on
Tehran radio in which he stated, "The brothers who rallied
on motorcycles all over Tehran against social vice had done
so with the prior knowledge of the Interior Ministry."
Rafsanjani's comment while he was preaching at Friday
prayers was, "We see now that these people need violence to
some extent" (Goodwin 1994:112).

But even this brutality pales into insignificance when
compared with a horrible practice that has been repeatedly

affirmed from various sources. Best-selling author Betty Mahmoody writes, "Whenever the *pasdar* arrested a woman who was to be executed, the men raped her first, because they had a saying: "A woman should never die a virgin" (Mahmoody 1987:293).

It is hard to imagine any religious sanction for such cruelty, but the rationale offered is that virgins will most likely go to Paradise. To make sure that these condemned women have no such opportunity, the jailers fulfill their lust at the expense of their horror-stricken prisoners.

Muslims living in the West also have been known to engage in violent behavior in order to be faithful to the tenets of Islam.

"In America, an Islamic extremist stabbed his sixteen-year-old daughter to death because she wanted to live a Western existence like her classmates. Palestinian-born Tina Isa, a St. Louis, Missouri, honor student died in 1989, four years after her family moved to the United States from a village near Jerusalem. Her father was outraged that she wanted to date a local boy and had taken a part-time job at a fast-food restaurant. When she returned home after her first day at work, her father claimed she had shamed the family's honor and for that she should die" (Goodwin 1994:301).

The religious police in Saudi Arabia are infamous for their harassment of women. Even the male members of the ruling family seem fearful that these religious fundamentalists might lead a revolt against the government. As a result, they have equipped these zealots with fleets of expensive cars to use in patrols, and they have generally maintained a neutral stance toward their restrictions on women.

An Australian nurse, Lydia Laube, who worked in Saudi Arabia, graphically recounts an incident that burned deeply into her soul. One morning she was instructed to gather her staff in front of the hospital's recreation center. Arriving in the open area, she observed hundreds of hospital workers who had been bussed in from adjacent towns. Her account of what happened next is truly terrifying:

"Then the *matawain* arrived, and I knew something unpleasant was going to happen...I saw several men pushing and pulling the Filipino tailor and his assistant out to a space cleared in the middle of the crowd...Then I saw a Filipino nurse, who had been standing with a group of other women, suddenly seized by two *matawain* and also dragged to the centre of the cleared space in the enormous crowd, which formed a big circle around the victims....The boys were pale and trembling. The girl was terrified and crying. The *matawain* produced a long, thin, bamboo stick. I went cold with terror as I realised (sic) that they were going to be whipped....

"By now the terrified nurse was almost hysterical. She was shrieking, weeping and saying, 'No! No!' The *matawain* held her firmly by the wrists with her arms extended. The third one with the whip intoned the list of her crimes, a reading from the Koran and an exhortation to Allah. On finishing, he raised his arm; the whip bent, and then cracked down on her back and legs. She screamed and would have fallen if she had not been firmly held.... The girl was given fifty lashes. I fought back waves of nausea. She appeared to be unconscious at the end and was carried away and admitted to the hospital for treatment of her wounds and shock. The two young tailors received seventy lashes each and were taken immediately to prison" (Laube 1991:160–163).

Some time later, the Filipino nurse was deported while the tailors remained in prison for six months. The crime was that the girl had simply passed on a video to her fellow countryman. The accessory to the crime was guilty of nothing more than being present when the video was given to the tailor.

Female contract workers are a special target of the religious police. These women come from countries like the Philippines, where relationships between men and women are casual and liberated. Suddenly they find they must adapt to an oppressive set of regulations. For many, the strain is intolerable. Some try to beat the system and end up in serious trouble. Others just call it quits and return home. They are the fortunate ones!

Laube relates another Saudi story, this time of an Indonesian girl.

"Once an Indonesian maid was brought in with a cut throat and multiple stab wounds to her chest, back, arms, face and even the top of her head. She was placed in intensive care in a terrible state and very nearly died. Her diagnosis was also attempted suicide. The cut throat and some stab wounds she could have administered, but she would have to have been a double jointed contortionist to have stabbed herself in the middle of the back and the top of the head with such force. This poor girl eventually spoke to one of the nurses who understood Indonesian, and she said that the master of the house regularly made advances to her and that she tolerated it when it was only sex, but had objected when he demanded of her acts that she considered unnatural. When she resisted he had attacked her, and then the rest of the family came and joined in the attack" (Laube 1991:155).

Sadly, another attempt was made on her life while she was in the hospital. When she was placed in her own room, someone came into her room and pulled the stitches from her throat wound, leaving it gaping open. The girl was restored, and the hospital placed a guard by her room until they could transfer her (Laube 1991:155). Even the family assisted in the cruel attack. A maid is a piece of property with no rights and no recourse to law. Within Muslim families, various sayings are passed down from generation to generation. These stories are not from the Quran, but they serve as an oral guide to motivate "proper" behavior. Anees Jung, a Muslim woman who writes about women in India, recounts the influence these words had on her.

"She taught me to pray, to recite the suras. In the evenings she would tell stories that I remember to this day. 'A woman will be punished if she shows herself before any man. Even if a hair is revealed, that hair would bear a snake in hell,' she would say. I used to go around hiding each hair under my veil" (Jung 1993:107).

Fatima Mernissi, a Moroccan Muslim feminist writer, shares an unforgettable incident from her childhood.

"One day when I was little and came home from the Koranic school with feet swollen by the *falaqa* (a device that holds the feet in place so that the soles can be beaten), my grandmother, who always tried to teach me how to be happy, asked me, 'But, little one, what exactly did you do?' I held back my tears of humiliation and started to formulate my answer: 'I wanted to say to the *faqiha* [teacher]...' And my grandmother, who had 50 years of the harem behind her, interrupted me before I could even finish my first sentence: 'Child, don't bother to go further. You committed a very grave fault. You wanted to say something to your *faqiha*. You don't say something at your age, especially to someone older. You keep silent. You say nothing. And you will see, you won't get any more beatings.' My grandmother died when I was 13 years old, on a beautiful summer afternoon. I grew up, developed broad shoulders, left the Koranic school, and went out into the world with a sure step in search of dignity. But my progress has always been interrupted by the dismayed advice of those who love me and wish me happiness. They always say the same thing: you must keep quiet if you don't want to be beaten" (Mernissi 1993:187-188).

Mernissi has found that dignity. Her intelligence and drive opened the doors. But for millions of Muslim women, such an opportunity may remain a hopeful fantasy.

Female Jihad

At what point does an adherence to an ideology or religion metamorphose from a balanced dedication into a fanatical obsession? Adolph Hitler, as a student, wrote a Christian essay; Moses Berg (who founded the "Children of God" cult) was an evangelical pastor; David Koresh was an ardent investigator of the book of Revelation. At some point in time, these men crossed a crucial line, and devastating consequences followed.

Certainly, both Christianity and Islam have had their share of obsessed leaders and followers. Any religion that dogmatically asserts that its followers alone are on the true path to God and that all others are spiritually lost is set up to develop a fringe community. Ibn Warraq, in his riveting book, *Why I Am Not A Muslim,* piercingly critiques all theistic religions, asserting that their exclusivity causes some adherents to engage in religious violence. He documents his thesis with historical data, citing Judaism, Christianity, and Islam as proof texts. Warraq, who seems to be a sensitive academic, concludes that the only sensible path is to avoid all such pitfalls and become a secular humanist. To him,

Judaism and Christianity are as flawed as Islam.

With all due respect to this former Muslim and to Charles Templeton, who powerfully chronicles his journey away from evangelicalism in his book *Farewell To God, My Reasons for Rejecting The Christian Faith*, I still cannot accept their rationale. Yes, they do score points. Jihad, in some form or other, has sadly been found in all three theistic religions. I do not whitewash Judaism or Christianity. But, my contention is that Islam has a violent ethos that perpetuates itself generationally. It is based on the "inerrant" Quran and reliable Traditions.

Muhammad fought major battles, at the outset, in order to ensure the success of his religious revelations, and his adherents followed his commands and example. As we survey the world in this third millennium, we find Islam to be the major advocate of jihad. This has affected women as well as men.

An authoritative Hadith indicates that Muhammad approved of a Muslim woman who was ready to do violence to a polytheist. It reads, "It has been reported on the authority of Anas that on the day of Hunain, Umme Sulaim took out a dagger she had in her possession. Abu Talha saw her and said: Messenger of Allah, this is Umme Sulaim. She is holding a dagger. The Messenger of Allah asked her: What for are you holding this dagger? She said: I took it so that I may tear open the belly of a polytheist who comes near me. The Messenger of Allah began to smile" (Chaudhry 1991:128).

That type of permission from the Prophet has given inspiration and incentive to Muslim women throughout history. Even Aisha, Muhammad's favorite wife, led the battle for the cause of Islam.

Palestine is the contemporary cause célèbre for the Islamic

world. Muslims from different countries have joined voices, finances, and, at times, weapons to protest the Israeli "occupation" of their homeland. Young women have also been drawn into the net of violence. Imams have assured them, along with young men, that they will gain immediate entrance into heaven if they are martyred while performing jihad against the Jews.

Youthful Sanaa al-Muhaidli, a Palestinian young woman, blew herself apart by driving a car, packed with explosives, into an Israeli military convoy in southern Lebanon. She is considered a great patriot throughout the Muslim world. Her legacy is recorded in her own words in a letter that was released to the press after her death.

"My beloved ones! Life is only a stand of honour and self-respect. I am not dead. I am alive, and with you. O, how happy and joyful I am for this heroic martyrdom I have given....

"Do not cry for me for this courageous martyrdom. My flesh, scattered in pieces on the earth, will be once again, reunited, in heaven!

"Oh, mother! How happy I will be when my flesh leaves my bones, and when my blood surges into the soul of the South while I am exterminating those Zionist enemies" (Parshall 2002:280-281).

This has not been an easy chapter to write. How does one bring a proper balance to such a difficult subject? There are so many variables. Still, I must conclude that fundamentalist Islam has contributed to the oppression and pain of millions of Muslim women worldwide. Scattered throughout the following chapters, you will see many more instances of how this particular interpretation of Islam has impacted the daughters of Ishmael.

3

The Veil

At Cairo airport, the great crossroads of the Islamic world, it was possible to see almost every interpretation of Islamic dress. Women from Pakistan, on their way to jobs in the Gulf floated by in the deliciously comfortable salwar *kameez*—silky tunics drifting low over billowing pants with long shawls of matching fabric tossed loosely over their heads. Saudi women trod carefully behind their husbands, peering from behind gauzy face veils and 360-degree coverings, called *chadris*—colorful crinkly shrouds with an oblong of embroidered latticework over the eyes. Women from Dubai wore stiff, birdlike masks of black and gold that beaked over the nose but left their luminous, treacle-colored eyes exposed. Some Palestinians and Egyptians wore dull-colored, floor-length button-through coats and white head-scarves; others wore bright calf-length skirts with matching scarves held in place by headbands of seed pearls. (Brooks 1995:21–22)

In the midst of a similar chaotic, yet colorful, scene, Julie and I sat with our daughter Lyndi, her husband David, and their two small children. We were in transit from Cairo to Beirut during our family vacation in the Middle East.

Lyndi's probing eyes fixed on a Muslim woman sitting nearby. Every inch of the woman's body was covered by cloth. She wore a black veil from head to foot, webbed cloth to conceal her eyes, white gloves to cover her hands, and dark socks to ensure privacy for her ankles and feet. She was the embodiment of the twenty-first century conservative Islamic woman. After pensively staring at her for several minutes, Lyndi just shook her head and said, "How can a woman ever agree to be dressed like that?"

That is the question that I will explore in this chapter. The veil is perhaps the most controversial issue facing Muslim women today. This piece of cloth embodies the debate over liberation or subjugation. Most Muslim women square off on one side or the other. And of course men—husbands, fathers, politicians, presidents, and kings—are opinionated and vocal with their positions as well.

Unni Wikan, author of *Behind the Veil in Arabia,* wrote two succinct sentences that capture his emotional response to the veil.

"No matter how adequate my understanding of the burqa [full-body veil], I have never ceased to regard it, as an outsider, with a mixture of feelings: incredulity, repulsion, enchantment, and admiration...fascination. The burqa no doubt is one of the oddest pieces of material culture ever fashioned by man" (Wikan 1982:93).

Quranic data regarding the clothing of women is sparse, the most widely quoted Scripture on the subject is Surah (chapter) 24:31, which states, "And tell the believing women to lower their gaze and be modest, and to display of their adornment only that which is apparent, and to draw their veils over their bosoms, and not to reveal their adornment save to their own husbands or fathers or husbands' fathers, or their sons or their husbands' sons, or their brothers or their brothers' sons or sisters' sons, or their women, or their slaves, or male attendants who lack vigour, or children who know naught of women's nakedness. And let them not stamp their feet so as to reveal what they hide of their adornment."

The main thrust of this verse is to press for female modesty. Interestingly, the prior verse exhorts men also to lower their gaze and to be modest. Though it is commonly held that men should be covered between their navel and knee, the issue is hardly ever raised. One could make a case that the men are to be as rigid about lowering their gaze and being modest as women.

Abul A'la Maududi, the renowned, now deceased, Pakistani Muslim theologian, had to reluctantly admit that there is no Quranic basis that mandates the veil.

"A person who considers carefully the words of the Quranic verse, their well-known and generally accepted meaning and the practice during the time of the Holy Prophet, cannot dare deny the fact that the Islamic *Shari'ah* [religious law] enjoins on the woman to hide her face from the other people, and this has been the practice of the Muslim women ever since the time of the Holy Prophet himself. Though the veil has not been specified in the Quran, it is Quranic in spirit. The Muslim women living at the time of the Holy Prophet to whom the Quran was revealed had made it a regular part of their dress outside the house" (Maududi 1993:194–195).

Is the veil really "Quranic in spirit"? Modesty, yes. That much is clear. But isn't modesty culturally determined? In the early 1970's, I was shocked when I picked up a Pentecostal denominational magazine, and, while flipping through the pages, came to a picture of teenaged girls wearing very brief mini-skirts, standing outside a church. Each had a Bible. They were on their way to witness to the lost and tell them about a Savior who delivers from sin (and lust?). I assume they did not feel they were being immodest according to the norms of the day. But certainly there is a place for disagreement on that point.

Muslim theologians and authorities make a plea for a dress standard that will assure female modesty for all times and all places. It will be universal in design. No doubt, no questions, and no place for cultural relativity. The complete veil meets this requirement with room (or cloth) to spare!

Yvonne Haddad did a survey of women living in Egypt, Jordan, Oman, Kuwait, and the United States. She queried these women on why they preferred to wear the veil. Their responses were illuminating.

> Religious—an act of obedience to the will of God as a consequence of a profound religious experience, which several women referred to as being "born again";
> Psychological—an affirmation of authenticity, a return to the roots, and a rejection of Western norms. (One woman talked about the "end of turmoil" and a "sense of peace.");
> Political—a sign of disenchantment with the prevailing political order;
> Revolutionary—an identification with the

Islamic revolutionary forces that affirms the necessity of the Islamization of society as the only means of its salvation;
Economic—a sign of affluence, of being a lady of leisure;
Cultural—a public affirmation of allegiance to chastity and modesty, of not being a sex object (especially among unmarried working women);
Demographic—a sign of being urbanized;
Practical—a means of reducing the amount to be spent on clothing;
Domestic—a way to keep the peace, since the males in the family insist on it." (Zuhur 1992:105)

Quite a list indeed.

The Veil Defined

The word *hijab* comes from *hijaba,* which mean to conceal or to render invisible by use of a shield (Al-Munajjed 1997:47). Some interpreters believe this refers only to the hair of a woman, not to her face.

One level of controversy relates to women in the laboring class. Many imams would exempt them from wearing the veil. Such a garment would be unrealistic for a worker in the fields. The response of the fundamentalist, however, is that these women should be homemakers, not laborers in situations where their modesty could be compromised. I have observed this tension among rural Muslim women in Bangladesh. Economic necessity has driven them from the home to the workplace. Imams protest while husbands applaud their wives efforts to add to the cumulative family income.

Styles of Muslim veils vary significantly from country to country. Up to date, fashionable coverings can be found in a Cairo shopping center. Geraldine Brooks wrote about shopping for clothing options.

"Where women wore the veil, there was money to be made in Islamic fashion. Cairo had the Salam Shopping Center for Veiled Women, a three-floor clothing emporium that stocked nothing but Islamically correct outfits. Most of the store was devoted to what the management thought of as 'training hijab'—color-coordinated long skirts and scarves, long jackets studded with rhinestones and bulging with oversized shoulder pads—that covered the Islamic minimum. Ideally, explained one manager, customers who started wearing such clothes would gradually become more enlightened and graduate to dowdier colors and longer, more shapeless garments, ending up completely swathed in black cloaks, gloves and face veils. But these plain outfits, which cost around ten dollars, were hard to find amid the racks of more profitable 'high-fashion' hijab, where the cost for an Islamically correct evening outfit could run to three or four times a civil servant's monthly salary" (Brooks 1995: 22).

It is amazing to observe how religion and economics intersect. This store manager is able to make a profit off Muslim women, who, in the process of becoming more spiritual, "graduate" to a dowdier style of veil. But the real money is in the high-fashion clothes that are low in spiritual value. I wonder how different this is from the moneychangers and animal salesmen found in the Temple courtyard in Jesus' day? Or from the potpourri of high-price Christian books, CDs, and other assorted "Jesus" paraphernalia that is offered for sale around the world.

Others, like Hudda Khattab, have a more pragmatic view

on women's clothing.

"The clothing should not make you stand out—it should not be of such bright colours or way-out design as to attract attention. For this reason, some Muslims advise the Muslim women in the UK should avoid the more 'exotic' forms of Muslim dress—such as Arabian abayas or Iranian chadors (kinds of cloaks)—in favour of adapted versions of western dress, such as a skirt suit comprising a loose fitting, long-line jacket and long skirt of a smart cut. This is very much a matter of individual conscience, but this writer would advise taking the climate and one's field of work (whether inside or outside the home) into account when deciding on the type of Hijab to wear: what suits a stay-at-home mother with plenty of help in the house in Arabia may not be appropriate for a harassed working mother in rainy Manchester!" (Khattab 1993:16)

The mosque is a place of divine appointment. Worshipers come to meet God. Their demeanor and clothing must reflect this reality. In certain countries like Bangladesh, few women pray in the mosque. However, in the Philippines I have seen large numbers of women praying either behind the men or in the balconies of mosques.

A Muslim has shared his understanding of required modesty in such a context.

"The clothes we wear in the mosque must also be correct: all the body and hair—except the hands and face—must be covered properly, and no makeup or perfume should be worn. We shouldn't make the mistake of thinking that if our dress is 'Traditional Muslim Dress' it will be acceptable; shalwar-khameez, saris, long skirts and the like are not acceptable if they are tight or low-cut or reveal parts of the body such as arms, stomach or legs, etc. The intention in coming to the mosque should be to worship and to learn, not to show off or draw attention to ourselves" (Khattab 1993:2–3).

Some years ago, I listened in as a father urged his daughter, who was in her early twenties, to engage in her daily prayers. She looked at her dad and said with an air of exasperation, "I can't pray because I have polish on my toe nails." That ended the discussion.

There is a strange aberration to Islamic law and custom in regard to the veil. While visiting the country of Niger, I had the privilege to go out into the Sahara desert in a Land Rover and visit members of the Tuareg tribe. Firsthand, I observed what Brooks comments on.

"The oddest interpretation of Islamic dress I encountered was in the arid expanse of the Algerian Sahara, where the nomadic tribes known as Tuareg hold to the tradition that it is men who should veil their faces after puberty, while women go barefaced. As soon as they are old enough to shave their beards and keep the Ramadan fast, the men must cover all but their eyes in a veil made of yards of indigo cloth. 'We warriors veil our faces so that the enemy may not know what is in our minds, peace or war, but women have nothing to hide,' is how one Tuareg man explained the custom.

"The Tuareg are Muslims, but their interpretation of the faith gives women considerable sexual freedom before marriage and allows close platonic friendships with men after they wed.... Other Muslims find Tuareg customs close to heresy. In fact, the word 'Tuareg' comes from the Arabic for 'The Abandoned of God'" (Brooks 1995:22).

Surrounded by a sea of sand, tattered tents, and restless camels, I talked to Tuareg men who had all but their blood-shot eyes covered with dark blue cloth. This community of tens of thousands are truly nomadic desert dwellers. Though the Orthodox may question their pattern of promiscuity, still they rigidly maintain that their faith in Allah and the "Prophet of the Desert" is firm and unshakable. Few Tuareg have converted to Christianity. It would be almost unthinkable for any Tuareg woman to make an independent profession of faith in Christ. She is allowed freedoms non-existent for women in a country like Afghanistan, but still she is compelled to adhere to the Islamic faith. In one corner of the settlement, I noted prostrated, praying men. And so life goes on as it has for centuries.

Another interesting variation occurred in 1936 when Reza Shah of Iran began outlawing the veil. From a certain date all public transportation was denied to women wearing veils. Next came a dictum allowing only unveiled women to enter the market area. Another effective tactic was to demand that all registered prostitutes wear the veil. Quite naturally, decent women did not want to be mistaken for a prostitute (Voorhees 1988:86).

In recent history, women in Iran have worn the veil by choice, then the veil was outlawed by the government, and now it has been reinstalled as a mandatory covering. Tomorrow?

The Veil Appreciated

It is incorrect to assume that all Muslim women regard the veil with disgust. The following are but a few testimonies of those who consider the veil to be practical, protective, and even attractive. The veil hasn't always had such negative associations. Before Khomeini's rule of Iran, which lasted from 1979 to 1989, one woman's evaluation of veil usage was as follows:

"Veils, thus, are flexible. They are as well practical equipment against dust, in place of having to dress up to go out, for napping blankets, privacy in nursing, and so on; and adjusting them judiciously can be an effective flirting technique" (Fischer 1978: 208).

Needless to say, the flirting days are over, at least in the present climate of Iran. A twenty-nine-year-old single woman from Saudi, who spent most of her life in Europe, believes that the veil is not a sign of oppression.

"I think that it is very wrong to believe that the veil for the woman of Saudi Arabia is a sign of oppression or retardation or subjugation as the West believes...and it does not mean at all that we hold a secondary status as all the Westerners want to believe. These are all false assumptions built against us. I wear the veil, because for me it is a sign of personal and religious choice. It is because I lived in the West, and I saw all the corruption and immorality in their, as they call it 'liberated society' of illicit sex and drug abuse, that now I am more convinced of our local traditions and I am more attached to them. I want to preserve my Arab-Islamic identity, and for me, this is a way to show it" (Al Munajjed 1997:57).

This woman is highly educated with a master's degree in social sciences from a university in London. She has tasted deeply from the well of a liberated society. To her the water is polluted. Saudi Arabia, she feels, represents a social setting where she gains respect by wearing the veil. She has combined Arab identity with Islamic faith. Coupling religion and culture provides security and protection that is both attractive and satisfying.

But why is it that Saudi women are compelled to become anonymous in order to feel secure? How is it that a formless, seamless, colorless garment is required in order for a woman to be considered decent and respectable? Is wearing such a defense the only way that family honor can be preserved? Are Saudi men so uncouth, so brutal, so aggressive that the women need to retreat into multiple yards of stifling hot cloth in order to be protected? In Cairo, newspaper and magazine reporters surveyed girls who wore the veil. Some of their perspectives were published.

"'I feel comfortable and much more free in these clothes;' 'I wear the Islamic dress because it shows me to be a Muslim Arab woman, of which I am proud;' 'Many men treat women as objects, look at their beauty; the Islamic dress allows a woman to be looked upon as a human being and not an object'" (Hijab 1988:53).

As Julie and I have personally observed, there is a strong, pragmatic rationale in Cairo for wearing the veil or at least modest apparel. There are so many tourists invading Egypt adorned in what can only be described as minimal dress. Egyptian men look upon this as a sexual invitation, and not just from foreigners. The enticement also extends to Egyptian women if they are similarly attired. Elizabeth Warnock Fernea's comments reinforce this dilemma.

"Brotherly and sisterly terms of address are often used in work situations, suggesting that forms of mutual respect may be developing between men and women. But riding the bus and walking the crowded streets mean constant and often very close contact with strangers. One has only to observe the respect with which the modestly dressed working woman is treated in Cairo today to know how rewarding this must be after a few (or many) experiences of her being shoved, pushed, and often manhandled in short skirts, Western style" (Fernea 1985:291).

Another Muslim woman complained of a propensity toward fear. She decided to start wearing the veil. Excitedly, she reported that all her fears suddenly vanished and that now "there is nothing in this life that can frighten me" (Brooks 1995:158).

Fran Love, a former tentmaker in Indonesia, wrote about an American friend who did not comprehend the impact her clothing choices could have on her friendships with Muslim women.

"An acquaintance related an experience about inviting a Muslim woman to her home, not realizing that she would bring her husband. The woman acted cold all evening, not even attempting to make eye-contact or conversation. Puzzled, the American woman tried to guess why there was such a shift in her friend's attitude. Eventually it hit her: she had been wearing jeans, and had not changed into something more modest when the husband walked into her home. Her Muslim friend never returned" (Love 1996:136).

I am sure there are millions of Muslim women who do not protest to wearing the veil. It provides them with security and dignity, which they feel far outweigh any small inconvenience. But there are also millions who feel trapped in an antiquated seventh-century law that brings discomfort, embarrassment, and anger.

The Veil Denounced

Muslims have been known to blame Judaism and even Christianity for universal female subjugation. Nawal el Saddawi made some interesting assertions regarding the similarities between Christianity and Islam.

"Any serious study of comparative religion will show clearly that in the very essence of Islam, as such, the status of women is no worse than it is in Judaism or in Christianity. In fact the oppression of women is much more glaring in the ideology of Christianity and Judaism. The veil was a product of Judaism long before Islam came into being. It was drawn from the Old Testament where women were abjured to cover their heads when praying to Jehovah, whereas men could remain bareheaded because they had been created in the image of God. Thus arose the belief that women are incomplete, a body without a head, a body completed only by the husband, who alone possesses a head" (Saadawi 1980:5).

What can be said in response to such strong words? Definitely, many see clear traces of chauvinism in Biblical writings. Charges and responses abound. Modern day theologians apply diverse hermeneutical approaches to bolster their positions. But it does seem to be a bit of a stretch to declare that women within Islam are no worse off than those within Christianity and Judaism. Nawal El Saadawi even goes on to assert that Biblical ideology suppresses women even more than Islam does. Such striking words need far more proof than what Saadawi offers. Still, one can only sympathize with Saadawi's final statement. We are filled with cynicism as we read her interpretation that a woman is a body without a head. Veils are intended to show the inferiority of women and their subjugation to the male race.

Samuel M. Zwemer, the great apostle to Islam, writes, "In Arabia before the advent of Islam it was customary to bury female infants alive. Mohammed improved on the barbaric method and discovered a way by which all females could be buried alive and yet live on—namely, the veil" (Van Sommer 1907:6). Is it fair to declare the veil to be a "living death"?

Jean Sasson documents Saudi Princess Sultana's traumatic experience of first wearing the veil at age fourteen.

"The novelty of wearing the veil and abaaya was fleeting, though. When we walked out of the cool souq [market] area into the blazing hot sun, I gasped for breath and sucked furiously through the sheer black fabric. The air tasted stale and dry as it filtered through the thin gauzy cloth. I had purchased the sheerest veil available, yet I felt I was seeing life through a thick screen. How could women see through veils made of a thicker fabric? The sky was no longer blue, the glow of the sun had dimmed; my heart plunged to my stomach when I realized that from that moment, outside my own home I would not experience life as it really is in all its color. The world suddenly seemed a dull place. And dangerous, too! I groped and stumbled along the pitted, cracked sidewalk, fearful of breaking an ankle or leg" (Sasson 1992:95).

Sultana was fortunate to be able to put off wearing the veil until age fourteen. Iranian girls are mandated to cover themselves at age nine or younger, as Goodwin discusses in *Price of Honor.*

"Khomeini himself declared that joy was un-Islamic. Six months after the Iranian Revolution, he stated on national radio, 'There is no fun in Islam. There can be no fun or enjoyment in whatever is serious.' Certainly, that comment seemed to be taken seriously. The streets of Tehran look sorrowful the year round, with the predominant color being black, dominated by the women's *chadors.* I realized after a while that the only vivid color on the city streets came from the dresses of little girls. And because they brightened up the monochromatic cityscape, I found myself smiling at them, their bare arms and legs symbolizing a freedom soon lost. Legally, young Iranian girls must be entirely covered by the age of nine, although many are *chadored* long before then" (Goodwin 1994:106–107).

Muhammad is the model for all Muslims. By marrying

Aisha at age six, Muhammad paved the way for an enforced "protection" of young girls. This is accomplished both by marriage and donning the veil.

I tend to think that Khomeini thought that joy, fun, and enjoyment are equated with sin. He responded to the danger of a joyful society by taking steps to make it as bland and unattractive as possible. He succeeded in this during his oppressive years of rule in Iran.

Other "Guardians of the Faith" have taken up the mantle as Geraldine Brooks observed in a Muslim context.

"I had been in the emergency room of a Gaza hospital when a young Palestinian nurse came in, shaking, her uniform covered in wet, brown stains. 'It was the boys in the market,' she said. 'They told me to cover my head. I told them I was Christian, but they said it didn't matter. They said, "The Virgin Mary covered her head, so why not you?" They threw rotten fruit at me and told me next time it would be acid'" (Brooks 1995:155).

In Manila a young Muslim man told me with disgust that zealots were going around the nearby Christian market looking for any Muslim girls who were unveiled. If any were found, they were loudly denounced and told to put on some type of head covering immediately.

One evening I was listening to an extremely intelligent Filipino woman being interviewed on television. Her breadth of knowledge was impressive, as was her ability to articulate her views in pungent, colorful language. At one point the interviewer asked her to divulge her religious belief. With an unmistakable tinge of bitterness in her voice, she declared that she didn't believe in God. Somewhat taken back, the host asked her to elaborate. The woman responded by talking about her unhappy experience in a religious school. She said that the nuns were overly strict and domineering. They had no joy, only discipline. At an early age she had decided that if such demanding, unhappy people represented the Christian faith, then she wanted nothing to do with it.

So what do we conclude from all of this? Are there inadequacies within every religious system? Are there bad models that are set forth as representing God-ordained, absolute truth in all organized religions? Yes, of course. So how then do we make a fair evaluation of an issue like mandating women to wear the veil?

To the "veil enforcer," he or she is only following God-sanctioned guidelines for female modesty. Any potential for immorality is curtailed at the youngest possible age. "The law of Allah is all supreme."

Coming from a grace-oriented Christian tradition, I can only protest enforced spirituality. I decry immorality and all forms of rebellion against God, but the heavy hand of legalism can only lead to rebellion, in Christianity or in Islam. Prevailing love, as so beautifully presented in I Corinthians 13, seems to best represent what true religion is all about: "And now these three remain: faith, hope, and love. But the greatest of these is love."

4

Modernity

While sitting in a crowded waiting room in London's Heathrow Airport, I saw an attractive young woman dressed in tight pants and a revealing blouse. When it came time for our flight to Cairo to be called, I saw this Western-influenced Muslim woman don a shapeless black robe. No one could ever guess that a lively temptress dwelt underneath those yards of nondescript cloth.

Thirty minutes into our flight, the TV monitor switched on, and the religiously conservative as well as the liberal were treated to a video of scantily dressed men and women engaged in lively disco dancing. And this on Egypt Air! Perhaps more than any other nation, Egypt epitomizes the conflict between traditionalism and modernism. There are probably more mosques in Cairo than in any other city in the world. Al Azhar mosque and university stand as guardians of the faith. The Brotherhood lashes out against everything they consider anti-Islamic. Veiled women abound.

On the other hand, raunchy discos with nearly nude belly dancers are easily located. Prostitutes prowl the streets, particularly seeking out rich Arabs from nearby fundamentalist countries. Many Egyptian women are dressed in knee length skirts, and foreign women in tight shorts are tolerated.

Nawal El Saadawi, Egypt's leading feminist, has shared some of this conflict in her writings as recorded by Christine Mallouhi.

"I hated my femininity. I felt that it was chains. I hated the ugly limited world of women, from which emanated the odour of onion and garlic. 'Your future lies in marriage;' my mother repeated that word until I hated it. In my mind I connected the smell of the kitchen with the smell of a husband and I hated the word 'husband.' This long heavy hair that I carry on top of my head everywhere. It hampers me every morning, burdens me in the bath, and burns my neck in the summer.... But my mother rules over my life, my future, and my body even down to the locks of my hair. Why? Because she gave birth to me? I was imposed on her as a daughter and she was imposed on me as a mother. Is it possible for someone to love a being imposed on her? And if my mother loved me with a true love whose aim was my happiness and not hers, then why are all her orders and desires in contradiction with my comfort and happiness?" (Mallouhi 1994:60)

The chains of her womanhood led her to hate her femininity. She did what many Muslim women have done; she compared herself to a man. Why should men have all the freedom while the women languish in cultural, religious, and physical bondage? These types of questions are the very foundation of the quest for some measure of liberation. Equality. Choice. A liberated voice. These are words that are beginning to crescendo throughout the Muslim world. In certain places, only a whisper can be detected; in other countries the clamor generates decibels loud enough to frighten intimidated men. Author Jan Goodwin was visiting Khomeini's tomb in Iran during the anniversary of his death. She records one intriguing conversation she heard in her book *Price of Honor.* "A young woman nearby who had only her eyes uncovered...leaned over shyly to ask me in stumbling English where I was from and why I had come today. 'I am here only because our school bused us here. It was required,' she told me. 'The government pays for buses to bring people from the schools, colleges, factories. They even go to the villages. The factory workers get double salary to make sure they come.' Dropping her voice, she added, 'Otherwise no one would be here...well, many fewer than today.'

"Not sure if she had convinced me, she added, still whispering, 'Do you think I dress like this at home? No, of course, I don't.' And to prove it she flashed open her chador to show me her jeans and lavender T-shirt underneath. 'I hate it, hate all this. I am sixteen, this is my time, my youth, I should be having fun. Instead, I am here, dressed like a peasant grandmother, to mourn a dead old man who hated beauty, hated happiness. If God meant us to dress in black, if he meant us to have no color in our lives, why did he give us flowers? That's what I would like to have asked that dead Imam'" (Goodwin 1994:127).

"I hate all this." This sentiment has strongly reverberated across the Iranian landscape. Youth are quietly mobilizing, seeking to implement the second cataclysmic revolution to take place in Iran in our generation. This time there is no charismatic Khomeini at the helm. Rather, there are thousands of young people who are fed up with the overbearing tactics of the religious police. How much longer can their acts of suppression prevail?

A Muslim woman in America makes her plea for fitting in with the norms of Western dress styles. "How women dress outside of the mosque is their own private business. I don't want to go to college with my head covered. Wearing a short skirt does not make me a bad Muslim. I am a Muslim and I am proud to say it, but I want to say it in ways other than dressing in obnoxious clothing. I want to blend in as far as my clothes go. I want to look normal" (Haddad and Lummis 1987:133). Since this woman lives in the United States, it is understandable that she feels Islamic dress would be noticeable.

One young Muslim of our acquaintance was strict in wearing conservative dress in her own country. Never had we seen her attired in anything other than a sari or *salwar kamese*. It therefore was a bit of a shock to meet her in the States where she was attending an Ivy League graduate school dressed in a blouse and slacks. She was modestly covered, but by Western standards.

Another woman defines her position on prayer and worldliness. "'How will God accept your prayers if your face is always made up and you sit with men,' people ask me. I tell them as long as I do my prayers, I can paint my face, switch on the video and even watch a movie. There is no purdah between God and a woman" (Jung 1993:111).

There are more brash ways to be worldly than wearing make up and attending a movie. In a large-circulation Manila newspaper a picture appeared of the daughter of the Saudi Ambassador to the Philippines. She was participating as a model in a fashion show that was attended by the male and female elite of the Philippines. She was attired in a strapless dress. Her parents were beaming with pride. If she had appeared in that dress on any street in Saudi Arabia, she would immediately be beaten and taken to jail. One ponders the reason for the double standard.

Another anomaly is the red light districts that are found around Manila. I have seen many discos with advertisements printed in Arabic. These places are fronts for prostitution. It is a commonly accepted fact that Muslims from the Middle East are high spending customers in such establishments. Perhaps this is their way of gratifying their sexual appetites while at the same time protecting the morality of the female population of their home country.

Pakistan is a Muslim country in moral crisis. Fundamentalists are making their voice heard in laws ranging from blasphemy to street dress. Yet, the underground culture is replete with drugs, alcohol, pornography, and fornication. Friends in Pakistan have told me how pervasive the X-rated video traffic is. Young and old, men and women, meet covertly in homes to allow their salacious fantasies to roam where reality dares not tread. Goodwin comments on this in *Price of Honor.*

"She may leave home covered from head to toe, and in the company of a chaperon. Once she arrives at her destination and sheds her *chador*, she may be wearing a miniskirt, and she may exchange her chaperon for her boyfriend almost as quickly. In Pakistan, as in most Islamic countries, alcohol is illegal, but at private parties bootleg whiskey and gin are served, and she will be drinking. And in someone's home when parents and servants are away, her crowd will watch smuggled-in soft porn on the VCR. In Muslim countries where any physical contact between sexes or the display of a little flesh in movies is censored, the video industry has liberated many libidos. And just as in the West, her boyfriend may proposition her, and she may accept, having taken the precaution of stocking up on the contraceptive pill while she was abroad. And should she have the misfortune to become pregnant, she'll go abroad again, on the pretext of a shopping expedition, to have an abortion" (Goodwin 1994:68–69).

A more startling example of this conflict between the traditional and the liberated took place at a beach resort in Cyprus. A friend told me he was amazed as he watched a family who had come from a Muslim country to Cyprus for a vacation. On the beach the mother was dressed in a long black veil. Lying next to her was her teenage daughter with her breasts uncovered. This would certainly not be regarded as typical, but perhaps as a trend for the Western-influenced, nominally religious Muslims of the future.

Yes, without a doubt, the West is reaching out to the young Muslim girls of the world. But in areas of moral standards, we Christians experience nothing but shame. Liberty brings license. Sexual standards are destroyed, and consciences are anesthetized.

Conflict

When one engages in an ideological-cum-religious controversy with Muslims, one quickly discovers the intense feelings that prevail. Even in more liberated Muslim countries women are hitting the wall of revived fundamentalism. Often it is seen that leadership leans to the political wind. Whoever appeals to emotional religious sentiment is able to make the most impact on a president or a king.

In a country like Saudi Arabia, the sexes are segregated within the educational system by the time the student turns six. As there is a shortage of female teachers, closed-circuit television is set up in classes and the male lecturer teaches and responds to questions by intercom. When asked whether classes should be integrated, sixty percent of women respondents replied negatively (Al Munajjed 1997:36–37). I guess it is surprising that forty percent voted in favor of non-segregated classes.

For the Muslim woman who has decided to plant a foot on two divergent paths, personal conflict is inevitable. Cherry Mosteshar, an Iranian woman who grew up in America and then returned to Iran on a visit, writes eloquently of this struggle in her book, *Unveiled: One Woman's Nightmare in Iran.*

"When you grow up in another country with another culture, it becomes a matter of loyalty and pride to maintain your individuality, your own Persian—or whatever—identity. But you also grow up with your new society, you absorb parts of your new culture. You cannot help but become a hybrid. Then there comes a day when you are faced with the pure form of your first culture—in my case it was Muhammad— and you see things in your adopted home that conflict with it in the most fundamental ways. Yet to accept the latter is to betray the former. Before you realise (sic) it you are tearing yourself apart trying to be all things to all men, and most difficult of all to yourself" (Mosteshar 1996: 301–302).

Mosteshar's most interesting and challenging statement is that Muslim women who are exposed to a "new society" cannot help but become a hybrid. Old and new clash. To fully accept one is to deny the other. In her book, Mosteshar responds to this emotional dissonance by settling down in the middle. Islam is not to be denied, but rather than being an exclusive reality, this social and religious component of life is to be shared with the new "adopted home." The paradigm shift is from exclusive to inclusive.

Does this work when there is a Western cultural intrusion into a Muslim context? Conflict is imported through the World

Wide Web, cinema, videos, cable TV, print media, Western fashions, casual male-female relationships, and food preferences just to name a few. These forces can be insidious or bombastic. But, in whatever form they are found, no one can deny that they are at work. All too often it is Muslim women who are in the eye of the storm. And unfortunately, they seldom get the opportunity to set a direction. That prerogative lies in the male domain. Middle ground is but an ethereal fantasy for the multitude of women who are bonded into Islam.

Within Saudi Arabia, Geraldine Brooks observed women gently pushing against the norms.

"More and more educated women were competing for the few Islamically sanctioned jobs in medicine, education or women's banks. The banks, run by Saudi women managers and staff, had opened in 1980 because, although the Koran gives women control of their own wealth, Saudi segregation rules were denying them that control by effectively banning their entry to banks used by men. Even though daughters inherit only half as much as sons, in post-oil Saudi Arabia that often comes to a fortune. The new banks were meticulously segregated, down to women auditors to oversee the accounts of the female branches and guards posted at the door to see that men didn't enter by mistake. Usually a guard was married to one of the women employees inside, so that if documents had to be delivered he could deal with his wife rather than risking even that slight contact taking place between unmarried members of the opposite sex" (Brooks 1995:172–173).

How sad that the pragmatics of life militate against Quranic allowances. The wealth of women, in most instances, must be entrusted to male relatives, but it is at this point that violations occur. Few women would be able to protest inequitable treatment from a brother or husband.

Morocco is a North African, mostly Muslim country that has been incrementally moving toward modernity. A missionary who has lived in the nation for thirteen years shares her observations. She says, "Television has played a role in bringing changes to the attention of the public. Family planning has been advertised on TV for about five years now and invariably all the women who are seen on such advertisements are wearing modern dress. In the relatively short time of ten years our country has gone from one rather poor national TV station to the easy availability of recent American films, racy French programmes and soft porn."

Here is a country that has the potential of becoming modern or of sliding back into conservatism. Obviously Morocco is not dormant in a cultural sense. Will the Fundamentalists rise up with a clarion call and demand for the citizens to return to Islamic basics? Will a Khomeini-type leader captivate the masses as was done in Iran? Most likely, there will be ongoing tension as in Egypt.

How can Muslim youth circumvent the system? In the United Arab Emirates young men flirt with cautious persistence. "At the multistory Al Ghurair Mall in Dubai, groups of youths drop their telephone numbers at the feet of veiled women, or insert them into videocassette cases, in the hope that a woman will contact them. They also speed alongside vehicles driven by young women, flashing their telephone numbers at them on large pieces of board" (Goodwin 1994:146).

These attempts at circumventing Islamic prohibitions are fraught with danger. An imam may obtain the phone number from the video case and report it to authorities. The pretty young woman driving down the highway who sees a phone number flashed out of a passing car may use her cellular phone to call the police. Telephone conversations can be monitored on extension phones. What passes for normal interaction between the sexes in the West can lead to incarceration in a Muslim context.

Even before Ayatollah Khomeini came to power in Iran, the Shah laid the foundation for the subservience of the female sex when he stated, "In a man's life, women count only if they are beautiful and graceful and know how to stay feminine...and this Women's Lib business, for instance. What do these feminists want? What do you want? Equality, you say? Indeed! I don't want to seem rude, but...you may be equal in the eyes of the law, but not, I beg your pardon for saying so, in ability" (Betteridge 1983:115).

And so the conflict continues.

Protests

Taslima Nasrin is a name at once famous and infamous throughout Bangladesh. This well-known authoress was traumatized when, in 1992, Muslims in her beloved country conducted a brutal Jihad against Hindus. The savagery directed toward innocents was in response to Hindus who, in a terrible violation of religious sensitivities, destroyed the Babri Mosque in India. Nasrin, in a brief seven days, wrote a novel entitled *Lajja,* which was based on the facts surrounding the killings of Hindus in Bangladesh. Muslim fundamentalists went ballistic. In a reprint published by Penguin Books in India, Nasrin relates the persecution she has had to endure.

"*Lajja* was published in February 1993 in Bangladesh and sold over 60,000 copies before it was banned by the government five months later—their excuse was that it was disturbing the communal peace. In September that year a fatwa [a religious edict] was issued against me by a fundamentalist organization and a reward was offered for my death....But none of these things have shaken my determination to continue the battle against religious persecution, genocide and communalism. Bangladesh is my motherland. We gained our independence from Pakistan at the cost of three million lives. That sacrifice will be betrayed if we allow ourselves to be ruled by religious extremism. The mullahs who would murder me will kill everything progressive in Bangladesh if they are allowed to prevail. It is my duty to try to protect my beautiful country from them and I call on all those who share my values to help me defend my rights.

"The disease of religious fundamentalism is not restricted to Bangladesh alone and it must be fought at every turn....I will continue to write and protest persecution and discrimination. I am convinced that the only way the fundamentalist forces can be stopped is if all of us who are secular and humanistic join together and fight their malignant influence. I, for one, will not be silenced" (Nasrin 1994:ix–x).

A brave woman, indeed! For her courage she was declared persona non grata in the land of her birth. From abroad, she continues her battle against religious fundamentalism. Her protests have taken her emotionally and intellectually away from Islam to secular humanism.

While a visiting scholar at the Overseas Ministries Study Center (OMSC) in New Haven, Connecticut, I was invited to give a public lecture on "Muhammad and Jihad." The announcement of my talk was published in several Yale University publications. OMSC administrators were more than a bit concerned when Muslim Yale students called and requested permission to videotape my lecture. A compromise was reached that allowed several Muslims to come sit in the front row and make an audio recording.

Following my hour-long lecture, I somewhat apprehensively opened the meeting for discussion. Immediately, a retired Yale professor stood and, in strong language, questioned the validity of a religion that would so harass Taslima Nasrin. One could feel the rise in room temperature. The professor was sincere but seemingly insensitive to the Muslims in the front row. I was a bit surprised that a liberal, pluralistically oriented Yale professor would be so openly denunciatory. Fortunately the Muslim guests kept their cool and politely made their counter case about the need to defend the ultimate truth of Islam. They contended that books should not be written that directly or indirectly slander the actions of Muslims. And, so continues the turbulence.

Speaking out against the fundamentalists often comes at a great cost. The dean of medicine at Kuwait University had assassination attempts on his life because of his protest of the veil.

"Dr. Helal Al Sayer instituted the ban after seeing a student's veil dragging on a cadaver being dissected. "It is unacceptable and unsanitary," he said at the time. There was also concern that less talented or lazy students could have exams taken for them by brighter students by using the veil to hide their identity. The prohibition led to a strike by angry students, who described it as 'an interference with their personal freedom, which Islam guarantees.'"

Shortly after the doctor's protest, his car was blown up. Goodwin continues, "Then a month and a half later, while I was in Kuwait, the dean was targeted again. A twenty-pound bomb was planted outside the living room of his home in the Yarmouk area of Kuwait City on a Friday afternoon, the Arab weekend and a time when his family would be expected to be at home. The explosion killed the forty-five-year-old Iranian gardener of his neighbor...and destroyed another neighbor's Mercedes. Dr. Al Sayer's family members, who were in a different room at the time, were unhurt, but the dean of Medicine, who rushed outside after the large explosion, had the gruesome experience of finding pieces of the gardener's body, including his severed head, scattered throughout his yard" (Goodwin 1994:160–161).

How does religion that espouses high moral and ethical standards ever tolerate a power segment within its inner core to be so cruel and so brutal? How can Islam dictate the overturning of regulations that affect the basic hygienic standards of a prestigious university's school of medicine? How disturbing, how shocking is the unbridled force of a misguided faith. But perhaps my greatest disappointment is not with the actions of a fanatical minority, but rather with the muted voice of the majority. Where is the overwhelming protest of the events that occurred at Kuwait University? Silence. An acquiescent silence or perhaps a silence birthed in fear.

In November 1990, forty-seven Muslim women were chauffeured to downtown Riyadh. There some of the women dismissed their drivers and, with the other women as passengers, began to drive down a busy street. Soon a group of religious police stopped the caravan of cars. After a brief exchange of heated words, the cars and women were driven to police headquarters.

There it was determined that the women were from high-class families. They all had international drivers licenses they had obtained overseas. The women were professors and businesswomen. Some even had ties to the royal family.

After broad consultation, the women were released. But then came the response by the Fundamentalists. When the women returned to their work the next day, they found their office doors plastered with graffiti. Students refrained from attending their classes. Denunciations were made from mosque pulpits. Phone calls were made to the husbands, who were exhorted to divorce their "whorish" wives.

Soon the government made a move and suspended the women from their jobs and confiscated their passports. A new fatwa was issued that stated that women who drove cars contradicted "Islamic traditions followed by Saudi citizens." This ruling formalized the prohibition of women driving in Saudi (Brooks 1995:198–200).

The outside world soon received reports of this harassment. Non-Muslims could barely believe such extreme acts would occur in the name of the world's second largest religion. Especially is this true in that there is no explicit or implicit reference to the issue in the Quran. In fact, some Islamic jurists (outside of Saudi) point out that women "drove" camels in Muhammad's time and that this is the equivalent to the contemporary Mercedes. Though this incident occurred over a decade ago, Saudi women continue to be driven by chauffeurs.

A more liberated Muslim woman spoke to a newspaperman about the Saudi sexually segregated society. She wanted to know what Quranic basis there was for such societal restraints. His response jolted her. "'Nothing,' he said firmly. 'Nothing in the Qur'an mandates such practices. No, madame, it is custom and tradition in the Kingdom that prescribes this attitude toward women, not the Holy Book.'

He raised his hand in case I felt like interrupting. (I didn't.) 'I wish to say that my wife and I, like many Saudi citizens, see this present situation between men and women as a transition period, a phase that will, we hope, pass away slowly as our society develops and adapts to the world in which we find ourselves'" (Fernea 1998:341).

These words are a small ray of hope in a cave of stygian darkness. Muslim men must be in the vanguard of initiating change or it will never happen on a broad scale.

Nigeria is a country with a serious religious divide. Half of the populace are Muslims and the other half are Christians. Communal conflict has been on the rise. In this context Nigerian Muslim women have begun to voice protest against what they consider to be inappropriate Islamic social regulations.

The female revolution in Bangladesh is absolutely amazing. Even though this nation is not ultra-Islamic, Bengali women have mostly been subservient wives and doting mothers. Few rural women had traveled over five miles from their home. Almost no one had engaged in any kind of business or self-help program.

All of this is undergoing dramatic change, which in turn is bringing about social and religious conflict. A 1997 article in *Time* magazine documents the dynamics of this sari-clad revolution.

"One secret to Bangladesh's turnaround is 'microcredit,' small loans that are given without collateral. Social workers have discovered that a start-up loan of as little $20 can often be enough to rescue a family from starvation.... What makes microcredit so novel is that relief agencies have been making the loans almost exclusively to women. Creditors realized that wives are less likely than husbands to squander the money on gambling and alcohol. With financial independence comes courage. Emboldened by the little cash they have managed to tuck away...some Bangladesh women are challenging the Islamic tradition.... They are running shops, riding motorcycles, and insisting on contraception" (McGirk 1997:42–43).

The use of microcredit has become a controversial issue in several Muslim countries. In some areas, fundamentalists have destroyed the projects made possible by these loans, often sending families back into poverty. In other areas, religious leaders have issued nationwide decrees that exhort husbands to divorce their wives if they work (McGirk 1997:42–43).

It appears that it will be the "unruly" women of protest who will one day make a difference in the world of Islam. Until then, entrenched traditionalists will hold modernity at bay.

5

Heaven and Hell

Muslims, uniformly believe in a judgment day that leads either to eternal bliss or to everlasting "hell-fire." The Quran and Hadith offer no alternatives. Even the few brave souls in the more liberal wing of Islamic interpretation dare not digress from orthodoxy on this subject. There is an unwavering, clear teaching in their scriptures that makes for a basically airtight case for Muslims to either revel in a sensual Paradise or suffer horrible torment in a literal Hell. The issue before us is how do women fare in an Islamic eternity?

Heaven

Is the Quran explicit on the presence of women in heaven? Consider these verses:

> And whoso doeth good works, whether of male or female, and he (or she) is a believer, such will enter paradise. (Quran 4:124)

> Allah promiseth to the believers, men and
> women, Gardens underneath which rivers
> flow, wherein they will abide—blessed
> dwellings in Gardens of Eden. (Quran 9:72)

Muslim scholars unanimously affirm the presence of godly, obedient women in Paradise. There is, however, very little written about their state of being. We know significantly more about houris (more about them later) than we do about actual women who have died. My imam friends have assured me that women will have equal rights with men in their eternal abode. This view, unfortunately, does not hold up to exegetical scrutiny.

There is no Islamic scriptural warrant to suggest that women will know their husbands in heaven. Nor will they have a spouse. No sex, no pregnancy, no children. Scriptural silence presents a mystifying fog over the eternal state of half of all Muslims. Strange. Especially so in light of explicit details concerning the revelry that Muslim men will relish in Paradise.

A Muslim Arab quoted by Charis Waddy pensively contemplates the fleshly allurements of heaven.

"Today much effort is being spent to prove that Mohammed's paradise was only symbolic. Wise men explain away everything. But let me tell you this, I have lived my life faithful to God in this baking desert. I have avoided one earthly temptation after another in an effort to gain paradise. If I get there and find no cool rivers, no date trees and no beautiful girls to keep me company, I shall feel badly defrauded" (Waddy 1982:129).

It has always been a mystery to me as to how Muslim women deal cognitively and emotionally with the Islamic teaching regarding houris. These female creations of Allah are specially provided for the sexual enjoyment of Muslim men in Paradise. It is important to quote only authoritative sources regarding this controversial subject, so I limit my citations to the Quran and Al Bukhari Hadith.

Houris in the Quran

"Which is it, of the favours of your Lord, that ye deny?— Fair ones, close-guarded in pavilions—Which is it, of the favours of your Lord, that he deny?—Whom neither man nor jinni [evil spirits] will have touched before them—Which is it, of the favours of your Lord, that ye deny?—Reclining on green cushions and fair carpets" (Quran 55:71–76).

These *houris* will be virgins when they receive the Muslim who first enters Paradise. Not even a jinn will have been able to cast any evil influence upon them. They recline on lush cushions and carpets awaiting their lovers. No person or force can deny this favor to a faithful Muslim man.

> And (there are) fair ones with wide, lovely eyes, Like unto hidden pearls. (Quran 56:22–23)

> Lo! We have created them a (new) creation And made them virgins, Lovers, friends, For those on the right hand. (Quran 56:35–37)

Pearls are highly valued by Muslims, thus this metaphor to describe beauty. Being "fair" relates to skin tone, which can bring a huge dowry to the female side of the family in the Middle East and Asia. Virginity is an imperative for marriage. Houris meet this requirement, along with being lovers and friends. Implied is the absence of quarreling, jealousy, or withheld sexual favors.

> This is a reminder. And lo! For those who ward off (evil) is a happy journey's end, Gardens of Eden, whereof the gates are opened for them, Wherein, reclining, they call for plenteous fruit and cool drink (that is) therein. And with them are those of modest gaze, companions. (Quran 38:50–53)

Everyone anticipates a favorable conclusion to the journey. The faithful Muslim male has it all. After the struggle of the Arabian Desert, he can now look forward to gardens that resemble Eden, with gates that are never closed. Fruit that has been scarce will now be found in abundance. The cool drink, we are told elsewhere, will be refreshing and non-intoxicating wine.

In Paradise, houris will be the companions of choice. Their modest gaze indicates singularity of ownership. Faithfulness to their husbands will be their duty and privilege. The proof text for marriage brings us to our next Quranic passages.

> Lo! Those who kept their duty dwell in gardens and delight, Happy because of what their Lord hath given them, and (because) their Lord hath warded off from them the torment of hell-fire. (And it is said unto them): Eat and drink in health (as reward) for what ye used to do, Reclining on ranged couches. And We wed them unto fair ones with wide, lovely eyes. (Quran 52:17–20)

They made it. Hell-fire has been avoided. The gardens of Paradise are their delight. Eating and drinking are joyous occasions. Good health is a coveted reward for obedience and faithfulness to God. And now to the wedding.

> Lo! Those who kept their duty will be in a place secure Amid gardens and water-springs, Attired in silk and silk embroidery, facing one another. Even so (it will be). And We shall wed them unto fair ones with wide, lovely eyes. (Quran 44:51–54)

It is important to understand the "We" refers to Allah. This Arabic figure of speech does not indicate plurality, but rather royalty. Clearly, God initiates the weddings of His obedient servants. The highest authority in the universe is making an absolute and indisputable statement of fact. Muslims will be married to "fair ones with wide, lovely eyes." These houris are Allah's gift to the men of Islamic society.

Our interest is piqued. Where did these heavenly damsels come from? How old are they? What exactly do they look like? How tall are they? How many houris go to each Muslim? If multiple, how is jealousy avoided? What is their behavior like?

Much has been written about houris within Muslim literature. Some is speculative and some outrageous. Other assertions can be considered authoritative. I choose to record only that which emanates from Al Bukhari's collection of Traditions. I have never met a Muslim who has disputed any of the following Hadith. Herein we find a commentary and extrapolation of Quranic material.

Houris in the Traditions

> Their wives will be houris. All of them will
> look alike and will resemble their father Adam
> (in stature, sixty cubits tall). (4:343; 55.1.544)

It is commonly understood that the wives referred to here will be the houris of the new creation in heaven. Interestingly, there will be no variety among these females. At first I was a bit shocked by this assertion. Males throughout the world are acknowledged to be appreciative of physical diversity in females. But as I mentally reviewed all I have ever read about houris, I cannot remember ever having read of any physical variations among them. This is particularly intriguing since Muslim men marry at least two houris each.

Fortunately this Hadith goes on to explain exactly how a houri resembles Adam. Where do we find in the Quran that Adam was ninety feet tall? Nowhere. Basically my Muslim acquaintances relegate this Hadith to the realm of mystery. They are hesitant to declare this a falsehood even though there is no confirming Quranic data.

And so we read that the houris are ninety feet in height. One can only speculate as to how tall Muslim men are in Paradise. Another Hadith describes the houris thusly:

> The Prophet said, "If a houri from Paradise
> appeared to the people of the earth, she would
> fill the space between Heaven and the Earth
> with light and pleasant scent and her head
> cover is better than the world and whatever is
> in it." (4:42; 52.6.53)

Light and perfume radiate from houris. The extravagance

of these qualities is seen by how they permeate all that is between heaven and earth. Head coverings for women continue to be highly valued in Paradise.

The most exotic and esoteric Hadith in regard to houris is as follows.

> Allah's Apostle said, "The first batch (of people) who will enter Paradise will be (glittering) like a full moon; and those who will enter next will be (glittering) like the brightest star. Their hearts will be as if the heart of a single man, for they will have no enmity amongst themselves, and everyone of them shall have two wives, each of whom will be so beautiful, pure, and transparent that the marrow of the bones of their legs will be seen through the flesh. They will be glorifying Allah in the morning and evening, and will never fall ill, and they will neither blow their noses, nor spit. Their utensils will be of gold and silver, and their combs will be of gold, and the matter used in their censers will be the aloes-wood, and their sweat will smell like musk." (4:307–8; 54.7.469)

Muhammad introduces his brief commentary by highlighting the fact that males will the first ones to enter Paradise. Why not females in the first two groups? Again we see the value of light, as these men will glitter like a full moon and the brightest star. In recognition of the fact that in our earthly pilgrimage there is often strife and enmity, Muhammad assures that these negative qualities will be absent in Paradise.

This passage also mentions that men will have more than one wife. Other less authoritative traditions have Muhammad assuring the male elect that they will each enjoy seventy houris, but perhaps this record is but a salacious fantasy of some writer of ancient days. The two wives, however, are a promise beyond dispute. They will be pure and beautiful.

The enigma of the houri's transparent flesh through which can be observed the marrow of her leg bones seems beyond the reach of even the most mystically oriented commentator. We will, therefore, leave it in the realm of the speculative.

Houris will be engaged in worship day and night. Body secretions are regarded as unclean, therefore these heavenly beauties will be free of such imperfections. Illness will also be absent from them. Utensils and combs will be made of extravagant materials. Their incense burners will be filled with the sweet smell of aloes wood. Bodily sweat will have the fragrance of musk.

Muhammad adds other details concerning these houris and their eternal residence.

> Allah's Apostle said, "In Paradise there is a pavilion made of a single hollow pearl sixty miles wide, in each corner of which there are wives who will not see those in the other corners; and the believers will visit and enjoy them. And there are two gardens, the utensils and contents of which are made of silver; and two other gardens, the utensils and contents of which are made of so-and-so (i.e. gold) and nothing will prevent the people staying in the Garden of Eden from seeing their Lord except

the curtain of majesty over His Face." (6:374;
60.294.402)

In Manila we often find Muslim vendors selling pearls.
Because pearls are referred to in the Quran, Muslims greatly
value them. Paradise will accommodate a pavilion made from
a single pearl with a width of sixty miles. The four corners
will provide lodging for the houris. Secrecy seems to be
desired, as these wives will not interact with each other.
Muslim men will "enjoy" them, which is a euphemism for
sex.

The gardens of Paradise are likened unto the Garden of
Eden. Gold is prevalent. Allah is unseen because of a curtain
of majesty over his face. All references to heaven are positive,
especially for men. Paradise is presented as so sexually
compelling that the spiritual is overshadowed. This has led
some Muslim commentators to descriptions of Paradise that
go so far into the realm of male fantasy as to make all my
above quotes and comments seem rather tame.

Hell

There are seventy-seven allusions to Hell in the Quran. It
is always presented as a terrible place of punishment. All
non-Muslims will abide and suffer there throughout eternity.
There is some question about those who have never heard of
the "straight path" of Islam, but most Muslims would handle
the problem as Christians do, and regard it as an obscurity.
However, assuredly, Allah will judge fairly and justly. But
this in no way undercuts the imperative of propagating Islam
throughout the world. The Great Commission for Muslims is
mandatory and to be implemented with intensity and self-
sacrifice.

> Narrated Abu Said Al-Khudri: Allah's Apostle
> said, "When the believers pass safely over (the
> bridge across) Hell, they will be stopped at a
> bridge in between Hell and Paradise where
> they will retaliate upon each other for the
> injustices done among them in the world, and
> when they get purified of all their sins, they
> will be admitted into Paradise. (3:371;
> 43.2.620)

Not unlike biblical data, Muslim scriptures are not explicit on the state of believers between death and resurrection. What is clear is that few Muslims go straight to Heaven. Martyrs for the faith, those who die on pilgrimage, and children who die prior to an age of understanding constitute the select group who will enter Paradise upon death without having to undergo any type of judgment.

All other Muslims, male and female, must endure two tests of their faith and works. The first involves the use of a scale, which measures good deeds versus bad deeds. The other test is to walk over the abyss of Hell on a thin blade of a sharp sword. Righteous believers will make it safely across to Paradise. Sinful Muslims will fall into the raging fires of Hell and suffer there until their transgressions have been purified. This latter concept is similar to the Roman Catholic doctrine of Purgatory.

It is important to note that no Muslim who affirms the oneness of Allah and the prophethood of Muhammad will remain forever in Hell, regardless of the terribleness of sins committed while on earth. A future of eternity in Paradise is theologically assured to every professing Muslim.

The practical implication of this doctrine is that Muslims do not have assurance about their entry into Heaven at the time of death. Their response is "I hope so." But most do affirm they will eventually get there.

Quranic verses on Hell are graphic and shocking.

> But as for those who disbelieve, garments of fire will be cut out for them; boiling fluid will be poured down on their heads. Whereby that which is in their bellies, and their skins too will be melted. (Quran 12:19-20)

Jane Smith and Yvonne Haddad have researched key Quranic citations about Hell. Their observations are recorded in their book, *The Islamic Understanding of Death and Resurrection*.

"The Quran offers a number of rather specific indications of the tortures of the Fire: its flames crackle and roar (Surah 25:14); it has fierce, boiling water (Surah 55:44); scorching wind, and black smoke (Surah 56:42–43); it roars and boils as if it would burst with rage (Surah 67:7–8). The people of the Fire are sighing and wailing, wretched (Surah 11:106); their scorched skins are constantly exchanged for new ones so that they can taste the torment anew (Surah 4:45); they drink festering water and though death appears on all sides they cannot die (Surah 14:16–17); people are linked together in chains of 70 cubits (Surah 69:30–32); wearing pitch for clothing and fire on their faces (Surah 14:50); boiling water will be poured over their heads, melting their insides as well as their skins, and hooks of iron will drag them back should they try to escape (Surah 22;12–21) (Smith and Haddad 1981:85–86).

The Traditions are equally hard on the inhabitants of Hell, as this representative quote indicates.

> I heard the Prophet saying, "The least punished person of the Hell Fire on the Day of Resurrection, will be a man under whose arch of the feet a smoldering ember will be placed so that his brain will boil because of it." (8:368; 76.51.566)

Lest we as Christians overly react to these descriptions, it is important to remember the words of Jesus that depict Hell as a place of intense suffering. The book of Revelation expands this theme. Muslims and Evangelical Christians have generally accepted a literal understanding of their respective scriptures concerning Hell. There are some, however, in both camps, who seek to exegete a more symbolic meaning of these verses.

Women's Place in Eternity

Now, we come to the place of women in this horrific abode. One well-known Hadith quoting the Prophet, gives Muslim women much to ponder.

> Once Allah's Apostle went out to the Musalla (to offer the prayer) of Al-Fitr prayer. Then he passed by the women and said, "O women! Give alms, as I have seen that the majority of the dwellers of Hell-fire were you (women)." They asked, "Why is it so, O Allah's Apostle?" He replied, "You curse frequently and are ungrateful to your husbands. I have not seen anyone more deficient in intelligence and religion than you. A cautious sensible man

could be led astray by some of you." The women asked, "O Allah's Apostle! What is deficient in our intelligence and religion?" He said, "Is not the evidence of two women equal to the witness of one man?" They replied in the affirmative. He said, "This is the deficiency in your intelligence. Isn't it true that a woman can neither pray nor fast during her menses?" The women replied in the affirmative. He said, "This is the deficiency in your religion." (1:181–182; 6.8.301)

Upon seeing these Muslim women, the Prophet exhorted them to give alms. This act helped to protect them from the fires of Hell. Muhammad went on to make the startling statement that the majority of the people in Hell are women. This word carried even more spiritual weight as it was uttered right after the prayer of Al-Fitr. More than a little astonished, the women asked why there are more women than men in Hell.

Muhammad's litany of the sins of women include cursing frequently, ungratefulness to their husbands, intellectual deficiency, inadequate religious observance, leading others astray, and having menses that cause them to be unclean so that they can neither pray nor fast. As a proof of ignorance, Allah has mandated that it takes the testimony of two women to equal that of one man. All of this conclusively states that over half of the Muslim population of the world has a serious "deficiency of religion" that will cause them to go to Hell, at least until their sins are purged.

Does not this authoritative saying of Muhammad set a theological and pragmatic groundwork allowing the deprivation of women's human rights? It is not right to condemn all Muslim women by declaring them to be unclean because of something that is beyond their control. Incidentally, this event is that which allows children to be birthed, and thus permits the ongoing growth of the Muslim world.

My friends have sought to explain to me, in vain, why the testimony of two Muslim women equals that of one man. Upon realizing the fallacy of any rational argument, they turn to God's sovereign will as the ultimate faith response to any of life's problems, be it in the theoretical or practical realm.

In the interest of fairness, it must be stated that a woman's period in Old Testament times left her branded as unclean for various functions of life. Menstruation is referred to as an illness. More contemporarily, as an example of deferred human rights, women in America were only given the right to vote in the 1920's. Was this not a statement of their inferiority?

Without doubt, women have suffered in every culture and in every historical period. Perhaps my major problem with Islam is how a Hadith like this gives the imprimatur of Allah to debase the female sex. Updating any interpretation of Islamic scripture is regarded as blatant heresy. Therefore, deprivation is assured.

Heaven and Hell. Both eternal abodes are defined as actual places. But does this Islamic teaching radically affect Muslim behavior? Probably not much more than the Christian doctrines of Heaven and Hell affect the 1.8 billion people who profess faith in Jesus Christ. Yet it is important for us to understand this teaching because of how it affects the perception of women in the Muslim world.

6

Folk Practices

Sima, an attractive, young, vivacious, Muslim mother of two boys explained to Julie and me the profound effect that going to Mecca had on her. The year before, she and her soft-spoken, engineer husband had performed this Islamic ritual, though it was not at the time of the annual Haj. Both Sima and her husband grew up in Pakistan but now reside and work in the States. Sima is a practicing anesthesiologist and surgeon. She has been immersed in the academic disciplines of science. Empiricism, rationality, and validated theories make up her life.

Enter Mecca. Sima told us about their stay in a five-star hotel that overlooked the mosque and Kaaba. She said it was a gripping sight to gaze upon. The hotel lobby and the streets beyond were filled with an awesome hush. They had arrived in the holiest city on earth. Allah's presence was palpable.

Soon this sophisticated, intelligent couple was in the crush of a great crowd, silently making their circumambulations around the Kaaba. Sima had her focus on one point in the huge courtyard. Her desire was to kiss, or at least touch, the protective covering behind which lay the holy stone that had been sent by Allah to Mecca. Finally, she reached the spot and, extending her hand over the heads of countless pilgrims, succeeded in the magic touch.

Sima said she felt a permeating sense of God's presence. She had come as close to Allah on earth as is humanly possible. There was no place for intellectual queries.

But doesn't this look like blatant idolatry? Aren't these Muslim masses connecting with God through a stone? Has our doctor friend set aside her rational faculties in favor of blind, irrational faith?

For Sima, however, this pilgrimage was life changing. She feels more holy. Her prayers are now regular. Allah is the center of her life. Her face glowed with serenity and contentment as she spoke. To her, faith had crossed the threshold into reality. Such is the inscrutable nature of connecting with the numinous.

Islam propagates a strict set of doctrines and rituals. But the outworking of faith for the average Muslim looks more like Folk Islam than it does orthodox belief and practice. Through illustrations, I will seek to elucidate this popular style of faith among Muslim women.

To some extent, Folk Islam is liberating. Women are free to participate as well as to be practitioners of a more unstructured style of belief. The focus of faith is experiential rather than legalistically binding. Within this matrix, the Muslim woman finds an outlet that is emotionally satisfying. Her personhood is validated. Islamic rituals are followed minimally or, in some cases, completely ignored.

Bevan Jones, author and missionary to India, reflects on the new status Muslim women receive upon return from the Haj.

"Women who have returned from the pilgrimage are looked upon as specially devout and go by the name of Hajni, Hajin, or Hajin Bibi. They make house to house visitations, read the Quran and instruct the womenfolk. Frequently they have brought with them clay from Mecca or Karbala [a place of Shiite pilgrimage in Iraq], flowers, zam-zam water, [from the Zam Zam well in Mecca which Muhammad reportedly drank from] or rosaries, and they sell small quantities of these treasures to the women for a few annas. These commodities are kept for use during illness; the zam-zam water is given to drink, and the clay is used to counteract pain and at childbirth. These women, also, receive rewards in the form of payment or food" (Jones 1941:258–259).

In North Africa some women practice a style of dancing that is believed to cause them to be inhabited by religious spirits. This is considered a worthy pursuit. Only females are present in these sessions. Emotions (and even sexual suggestion) are at a high pitch. Bill Musk wrote about this in *The Unseen Face of Islam.*

"As the music shifted, and different women moved to their feet and finally to their backs, the dancing was distinguished in the actions they made just prior to sinking to the ground in a trance. Some of their dancing was wild...as if the women had pent-up energy that simply had to be released. One spinster had a possessing spirit called the Prophet. The others liked her to dance early because she entertained them so well. Though unmarried, she writhed in an obviously sexual way, gliding slowly, head back, round the room, as if pressed against by the spirit. Another younger woman danced very intensely, though with hardly any movement at all. Her spirit was Yarwa Bey, and she slowly gyrated, shaking with heavy sobs, tears streaming down both cheeks, until she collapsed, crying, on a cushion. That afternoon, nearly everyone danced" (Musk 89:114).

Another Folk expression relates to the value of the blood of animals sacrificed to Allah. This is common throughout the Islamic world. In Morocco one missionary observed "women bespattering themselves with the first drops of blood that have oozed from the sacrifice, treading on the blood, entering their rooms and placing blood on the walls" (Fisk 1951:78).

Noted author Elizabeth Fernea related this incident that occurred when she, her husband Bob, and their servant girl Aisha were visiting a saint's annual death celebration in Morocco. Elizabeth said Aisha took her handkerchief and blotted up a bit of the spilled blood from a sacrificed camel.

"'It's baraka,' said Aisha, folding her dust and blood-besmirched handkerchief and tucking it carefully into her *djellaba* pocket. 'It's for Najiya. [Aisha's friend.] Maybe it will help her headache; we've tried everything else'" (Fernea 1980:275).

Baraka means blessing. It carries with it the idea of power. There can be transference of baraka from a spirit-filled inanimate object to a human. Its application, internally or externally, can bring healing, childbirth, or financial blessing. The aforementioned water from the Zam Zam well in Mecca is said to be power-charged with baraka. This is why it is sought after and exported throughout the Muslim world.

Folk Islam in the Philippines

Some good friends of ours, Richard and Marilyn, lived with a Muslim family, who was heavily involved in Folk Islam, for seven months in the Philippines. Marilyn insightfully shared with me some of her interactions with the woman of the family. For five years her husband had suffered from a heart enlargement. In desperation, the family went to a witch doctor who informed them that he was possessed by a woman of the clouds. This spirit wanted this man to be her spouse. The witch doctor told them this spirit was clutching his heart and refused to let it loose until the family allowed him to go and be with her.

Marilyn told me that in an effort to please this spirit, the family sacrificed a colorful rice and egg tray to her in the back yard. At the spirit's request, they uprooted a very old mango tree and pulled down a recently built kitchen area. (The family still won't build on that side of the house.) When the sick husband went into a trance, Marilyn said he spoke in a woman's voice. In the hospital, the spirit again spoke from his mouth, saying that in three days she would be back to get him. Three days later he died. The wife said the spirit-woman now had him.

"I asked her where these spirit priests get their power to predict the future and diagnose problems," Marilyn told me. "She told me it was from the evil ones. I then asked her why she, a woman of God, as she called herself, would go to the evil ones for advice and healing. She simply looked at me and said, 'It works.'"

In this instance the witch doctor was a last resort. The family had tried medical doctors but received no help. Now they entered into a relationship with a spirit who wanted to possess the husband. There was an understanding of the dynamics of the spirit world, but the family was helpless to overcome the evil forces at work.

This woman did not seem to have a sense of religious contradiction. Pragmatism was the driving force. Her response to Marilyn indicated that she did not feel she had offended Allah by supplicating malevolent spirits to heal her spouse.

Marilyn also told me about a ceremony in which a Muslim baby was "baptized." Marilyn said the Philippine Muslims contextualize the word *baptism* and use it to refer to the ceremony when a baby is initiated into Islam. Marilyn's husband, Richard, and six-year-old daughter, Amy, went to one of these ceremonies as guests and observers.

She said, "The baby is held by a 'sponsor,' and the imam cuts the baby's hair. Some of the hair is placed in a glass of water to see the future, some is thrown to the wind, and some honey is placed in the baby's mouth to ensure a sweet life. Then a plate of rice, chicken, and eggs in the shape of a crocodile is put on the floor. The other children are called to sit around it while an older woman with a coconut husk of burning incense walks around the circle chanting and blowing smoke on the children. Then the children are given the signal to eat."

Richard asked the father of the child why they were performing this ceremony. The parents had been educated at the prestigious University of the Philippines in Manila, and their family was very wealthy. He was the barrio captain. The father told Richard that he didn't know what it all meant, but they do it just in case it might help their child in some way.

Why was this ritual performed? "Just in case" was the driving rationale. All of the bases must be covered. Even an imam participated. For him, Folk practices do not conflict with his understanding of orthodox Islam.

Superstitions

In Oman there is an empowered mosque that people must respect, or else pay the consequences. A friend reports an often-repeated story. "A lady took something from the mosque—a gift that had been left for the mosque itself. As she walked away, she was struck with blindness. As she looked back towards the mosque she was able to see, but if she faced any other direction she couldn't see. She returned the item and her sight was restored."

Myth or fact? No one knows for sure. But the story itself presents a powerful incentive to avoid stealing from the mosque.

A friend told me two stories, both which come from the Emirates. She said an acquaintance, Emira, suspected her mother-in-law, who is from India, of placing a curse "packet" under her bed mattress. This packet was just a wad of folded and bound paper, containing a chart of random numbers. "Emira called a friend to find out how to break the curse. She had her daughter urinate on it, then she laid it in a trickle of water that carried it away from the house."

Defiling the packet broke the curse. It was rendered impotent by urine falling on its surface, and then it was expelled from the home. Numbers are often believed to be a conduit of evil influence.

My friend also said that in the Emirates, when people drink coffee, they leave the fine coffee grounds in the bottom of the cup. Then the cup is turned upside down on its saucer until the grounds dry. "A woman who knows how to 'open' coffee cups will look at the patterns that the dried coffee grounds make on the inside of the cup and tell the person what they say."

Reading coffee grounds is a well-known method of discerning future events, not unlike palm reading. Only a trained practitioner knows how to interpret this configuration of coffee grounds. Countless Muslims have unshakable faith in this and similar rituals.

Jinn

Followers of the Prophet exercise a strong belief in jinn. Such spirit beings can be benign or frighteningly evil. In many instances, jinn are presented as instruments of temptation. There is a well-known jinn in Morocco who goes by the name A'isha Qandisha. She seeks to seduce men. If a man capitulates to her charms, then he forever becomes her slave. The way to resist such a tragic consequence is to plunge a steel knife into the ground, and break her spell over him. In Algeria, a similar jinn-spirit is known as Betjallal. The name in Arabic means "lady of splendor." More than a few Algerian men believe they are married to this jinn and experience sexual intercourse with her (Musk 89:39).

To the outsider, such a belief is mythical, even amusing. But to the believer, jinn are a reality—usually to be feared. These spirit beings are frequently the instruments of some type of evil or destruction. In Morocco and Algeria, female jinn are usually presented in a seductive mode. Obviously, there is a strong psychological force at work in the mind of a man who fantasizes a sexual relationship with a spirit. One can imagine what wives of the indwelt men would experience. There would be jealousy, fear, and disgust.

In other areas, women have an inordinate fear that jinn will attack and kill their babies if their crying attracts the jinn's attention. This jarring illustration, reported by Unni Wikan in *Behind the Veil in Arabia,* comes from Oman.

"To reduce the risks caused by the baby's crying, mothers adopt a variety of measures; breast-feeding on demand is one response; the baby's wearing of amulets and branding with a hot iron (wasum) are others. But the most popular technique, applied twice daily, is to drug babies with an opiate, soukour. This is made from sugar and the dried flower of the poppy and thus contains morphine.

"From birth, the baby is fed soukour, once in the morning and once in the afternoon (for some babies, it is the first "food" they ever taste). The amount given increases with time, from a dose that covers the small fingernail, to one that covers the nail of the index finger, to a maximum dose that covers the thumbnail. Occasionally, this normal maximum may even be exceeded.

"The mothers know full well that soukour is addictive....Yet they do not consider the practice harmful, in view of its many beneficial effects. Protecting the baby from the jinn and stomach pains are some, leaving the mother in peace and with time to carry out her tasks and visit with the neighbors are others. We suspect, however, that there is a third, highly important one: ...their own extreme aversion to noise. The world should be a quiet place, people tactful and predictable, movements silent and gentle" (Wikan 1982:76–77).

It is sad how belief in a concept such as jinn can lead mothers to drug their babies. This is done with the knowledge and approval of the fathers. More threatening than the risk of addiction is allowing the child to become vulnerable to the wiles of evil jinn, or so says conventional wisdom among many in Oman.

Evil Eye

Another powerful force in the lives of Muslim women is the evil eye, a curse feared by most Muslims. Muhammad once gave the diagnosis and treatment for a girl who suffered with this affliction.

Narrated Um Salama that the Prophet saw in her house a girl whose face had a black spot. He said, "She is under the effect of an evil eye, so treat her with Ruqya (exorcism)" (7:426; 71.35.635).

Muhammad does not go into detail as to the ritual of exorcism, but this Tradition authenticates the practice.

Jean Sasson speaks of her Saudi princess friend as having a real fear of the evil eye. She is quoted as saying, "To ward off this, Arab babies are protected by blue beads pinned to their clothing. As enlightened as we were, our children were no exception" (Sasson 1992:189).

Mr. and Mrs. Bevan Jones, missionaries for many years to India, reported this story in their book, *Women in Islam.*

"In North India an English woman underwent a series of operations in the course of a single year. While in hospital she was visited by a Muslim girl-friend, a medical student, who gravely informed her that without doubt someone must have cast an evil eye upon her. The English woman remonstrated, but the other replied, 'Of course I know the causes of disease, but there never would have been need for you to have so many operations in so short a time had it not been that someone had put an evil eye upon you'" (Jones 1941:255).

Modern medicine, one of the most empirical of all sciences, at times capitulates to its antithesis: non-empiricism. Faith in the evil eye, a distinctly non-observable phenomenon, triumphs as the cause of many mysterious afflictions. Many educated Muslim women staunchly affirm this unseen, unproven "reality."

Spirit Possession and Exorcism

On a warm morning in a rural town of Bangladesh, we heard a loud knock on our door. A neighbor excitedly told Julie and me about an exorcism that was about to take place in his home. He cordially invited us to attend. Upon entering his living room, we saw a young girl writhing on the floor in agony. Saliva dripped from her mouth amidst grotesque sounds of grunts and groans; her arms and feet flung about in wild abandon.

A small group of sympathetic people stood gaping at the girl. The front door swung open and, with flair, the Bengali Muslim exorcist walked in. Recognizing him as a carpenter who had over-charged me in a recent project, I doubted his credentials as a man endued with spiritual power.

Immediately he took chalk and drew a tight circle on the cement floor surrounding the girl. Chanting the Quran, my carpenter friend took lighted incense sticks in his hands and blew the smoke into the girl's ears. Finally he breathed into her face.

The girl's writhing gradually came to a halt. The saliva dried up. Finally the girl fell in an exhausted heap on the floor. The exorcism was complete. The demons had fled. Normalcy returned. After receiving pats on the back for a job well done, along with a gift of *takas*, money, the rogue exorcist left the room, no doubt in pursuit of other demons and other tokens of appreciation.

My opinion is that the girl had an epileptic fit that gradually subsided. While not denying the existence of demons or the rite of exorcism, I do have doubts as to whether I had observed such a reality at that time. But then, in that room, there was a definite clash of worldviews. My bias was scientific and medical. Theirs was spiritual and faith-oriented.

An even more dramatic illustration took place in a rural area of Bangladesh. My close friend, Anwarul Karim, personally observed the following exorcism rite. Dr. Karim has a Ph.D. from the University of Dhaka and has been a

111

visiting scholar at Harvard University. He is not only a man of intense Islamic faith, but he also possesses significant academic credentials. Thus he, as an observer, combines both faith and rational in his chronicle of this event.

The possessed person was a beautiful young lady, thirty years old, who was married with two children. Her behavior had always been exemplary. She was very religious and modest. But suddenly she became abusive and would run around almost naked. Her fits included stomping on the floor and jumping from one place to another. In desperation, the family called in a *fakir*, Muslim holy man. Dr. Karim's account follows:

"The fakir was a middle-aged bearded man with a thick moustache and long loose hair. His eyes were sharp and penetrating. His teeth were broken and uneven. He was continually chewing betel leaf and occasionally puffing marijuana.

"The first thing he did was to look straight into the eyes of the patient. The moment the young lady saw the fakir she shrieked and went to a corner. The fakir had a small looking glass and a stone ring. He asked the patient to look through the magic glass, but she violently refused. The fakir then read a mantra and blew it over her. He again asked her to look through the glass. The woman made a sign that she could find an object in the looking glass. The fakir shouted at the top of his voice hurling abusive words toward the evil spirit who was believed to have possessed the village woman. His whole body began to shake and tremble. He recited some incantations taken from the religious books of the Muslim and Hindu community. He was using the names of Allah, Hari, Mahadev, Muhammad, Krishna, Fatima, Ali and Ma Kali. He drew a circle around himself and the patient. He then burned turmeric and asked her to inhale. He also brought an old shoe and asked the patient to inhale the smell. The woman refused and got violent. The fakir then hit her with a broom and followed this by putting hot mustard oil into her ears. The fakir was repeatedly asking the identity of the spirit. The patient refused to comply with the words of the fakir. Then the fakir burned mustard seed and read a mantra over it. This brought the desired result. There was a burning sensation all over the body of the woman. She agreed to talk. Below is the exchange of words between the fakir and the patient or the spirit who possessed her:

"Faqir: Who are you? Where do you live?

"The patient, with a strong nasal accent, said: I am Kalu, I live in the bamboo groves behind the house.

"Faqir: Why have you come into the body of this woman?

"Patient: She is beautiful. I like her.

"Faqir: Leave her immediately.

"Patient: No, I shall kill her husband.

"Faqir: I order you to leave her body.

"Patient: I shall not go.

"Faqir: See how I will force you to leave.

"The fakir began to mutter a mantra. Then he brought out a root of an herb which he kept in his bag. Meanwhile his associates started beating a tin can which made a roaring sound. The fakir also flogged her cruelly. She acquired much strength. Her hair was disheveled and her clothes were falling off her body. At last, she was forced to eat the root of the herb which she chewed and swallowed.

"The fakir said: Would you leave now? Have you seen I am more powerful than you?

"Patient: Yes, I will leave her. Don't torture me any more.

"Faqir: What sign will you make of your departure?

"Patient: I shall leave her. Don't worry.

"Faqir: Carry, with your teeth, an earthen pitcher full of water from the house and break it when you leave her.

"Patient: Yes, I will do as you order me.

"Then the woman, with her teeth, carried an earthen pitcher full of water and broke it after going five or six yards. Following this she fainted. The fakir quickly sprinkled water in her face. She was taken to a room where she slept for hours, after which she became normal.

"The fakir then asked the husband to make a sacrifice and to offer a small amount of money to a shrine of a Sufi saint that was known to the family" (Parshall 1989:169–170).

Certainly, this appears to be the real thing. But the interesting point is the ecumenicity of the ceremony. The fakir is a so-called Muslim holy man. His incantations, however, were a mix of Islam and Hinduism. This is not unusual when there is a Sufi Mystical element present. For us as Christians, there remains much ambiguity as we seek to understand such an encounter.

Muslim women in Pakistan who are harassed with demons go to a spiritual leader known as a pir in order to obtain deliverance. One such pir has a clubfoot, reputed to be a congenital deformity. His healing methodology was to ask the afflicted to lie down flat on the ground of his courtyard. Then he would hobble over them "curing the afflicted with each heavy step" (Naipaul 1998:338–339).

It has been noted that in Pakistan, victims of spirit possession are generally female and have a low socio-economic status. Widows and married or unmarried women who are experiencing domestic problems are also frequent victims. Married women who have a loving husband, understanding in-laws, and multiple children seldom have run-ins with demons (Chaudhry 1995:58).

Has there ever been research done on the male to female ratio for demon possession? Or the frequency among different ethnic groups and certain religious affiliations? My guess is that, across the board, there would be something like a 75 to 25 ratio favoring female over male spirit possession. Such a non-scientific estimate is based on my reading and anecdotes I have heard coming out of many countries. I leave it to the reader to ponder this hypothesis.

Shrines

Shrines are most often linked to a deceased Muslim pir. Usually his aboveground casket serves as a focal point for prayers and petitions. There is a strong Islamic tradition that the dead pir will intercede with Allah on behalf of needy supplicants. Women attend an annual festival at the pir's shrine in order to ask for assistance in finding a husband, getting pregnant, or meeting financial needs.

Women feel free to attend a pir's festival unveiled. It is felt that no man would molest a woman in such a holy place. Usually female devotees are prohibited from entering into close proximity to the casket. One reason for this is that the woman will become violently ill and feel as though her body is on fire. Another rationale is that the saint has supernatural powers that allow him to look through the clothes of a woman, and it is not proper to tempt a saint in such a manner (Jones 1941:311–312).

If women cannot go into the shrine, there is always a provision for them to pray nearby. They feel freedom to mix with men in close proximity to the holy area. I have never heard of or observed a women being violated in such a setting.

In one Sudanese village, a woman had been seriously ill for two months with a huge swelling of her neck. One night, even though experiencing a high fever, she dragged herself to a saint's shrine. What happened next has been recorded in the woman's own words by Bill Musk.

"'I was under the doum tree,' she said, 'with hardly sufficient strength to stand up, and called out at the top of my voice: "O Wad Hamid, I have come to you to seek refuge and protection...Either you let me die or you restore me to life; I shall not leave here until one of these two things happens...."

"'While midway between wakefulness and sleep I suddenly heard sounds of recitation from the Koran and a bright light, as sharp as a knife-edge, radiated out, joining up the two riverbanks, and I saw the doum tree prostrating itself in worship. My heart throbbed so violently that I thought it would leap up through my mouth. I saw a venerable old man with a white beard and wearing a spotless white robe come up to me, a smile on his face. He struck me on the head with his string of prayer beads and called out: "Arise."

"'I swear that I got up I know not how and went home I know not how. I arrived back at dawn and woke up my husband, my son, and my daughters. I told my husband to light the fire and make tea. Then I ordered my daughters to give trilling cries of joy, and the whole village prostrated themselves before us. I swear that I have never again been afraid, nor yet ill'" (Musk 1995: 184).

This story about a Muslim Sudanese woman offers hope to other suffering friends and relatives. In the shadow of the saint's tomb, she found peace and healing. Her experience validated her faith in the Quran, the shrine, and the saint. Needless to say, her witness is powerful.

Folk Islam has a strong impact on Muslim women. There are crosscurrents of peace, fear, spirit possession, exorcism, worship, granted and rejected petitions, freedom and bondage, and the known and the unknown. To millions of women this more mystical dimension of Islamic faith gives a hope and solace that strict legalism and ritual cannot offer.

7

Circumcision

Dr. Nawal El Saadawi, a Muslim Egyptian, shares her terrifying experience of being circumcised.

"I was six years old that night when I lay in my bed....I felt something move under the blankets, something like a huge hand...Almost simultaneously another hand, as cold and as rough and as big as the first one, was clapped over my mouth, to prevent me from screaming. They carried me to the bathroom. I do not know how many of them there were...All I remember is that I was frightened and that there were many of them, and that something like an iron grasp caught hold of my hand and my arms and my thighs, so that I became unable to resist or even to move....

"I strained my ears trying to catch the rasp of the metallic sound. The moment it ceased, it was as though my heart stopped beating with it...I imagined the thing that was making the rasping sound coming closer and closer to me. Somehow it was not approaching my neck as I had expected but another part of my body. Somewhere below my belly, as though seeking something buried between my thighs. At that very moment I realized that my thighs had been pulled wide apart, and that each of my lower limbs was being held as far away from the other as possible...I felt that the rasping knife or blade was heading straight down towards my throat. Then suddenly the sharp metallic edge seemed to drop between my thighs and there cut off a piece of flesh from my body.

"I screamed with pain despite the tight hand held over my mouth, for the pain was not just a pain, it was like a searing flame that went through my whole body. After a few moments, I saw a red pool of blood around my hips" (Saadawi 1980:7–8).

Dr. Saadawi cried out to her mother for assistance. Imagine her shock as she saw her beloved mother standing nearby, talking with and smiling at those who had just participated in "slaughtering" her daughter. A few minutes later, she saw her sister being carried away to the same bathroom. "The look we exchanged seemed to say: 'Now we know what it is. Now we know where lies our tragedy. We were born of a special sex, the female sex'" (Saadawi 1980:8).

Dr. Saadawi, at such a tender age, had become an unwilling participant in the centuries old ritual of female circumcision. There had been no emotional, physical, or spiritual preparation, only an act of painful mutilation. She was following in the tradition of millions of women who have encountered the knife under similar circumstances. When reading her comment, "we were born of a special sex, the female sex," one wonders if this is the only rationale to explain being traumatized for life.

In stark contrast to Dr. Saadawi, Aman, a Somalian woman, reflects on female circumcision and gives her conclusion in these jarring words.

"You know, I've heard many Europeans, many white people no matter where they come from, they're trying to educate Africans about circumcision. But would they accept it if I educated them to circumcise? This is my culture, my religion, and I don't believe another nation can take away another nation's culture. If Somali women change, it will be a change done by us, among us. When they order us to stop, tell us what we must do, it is offensive to the black person or the Muslim person who believes in circumcision. To advise is good, but not to order. These days in my country, they're doing it in the hospital so there is no pain. I hope more women will do it that way for their daughters" (Barnes 1994:280).

Aman is perhaps representative of many Muslim rural females who are taught that this is a mandatory religious ceremony that all females undergo. It is a natural rite of passage, not to be questioned or resisted.

Various Interpretations

There are different opinions within Islam concerning female circumcision. It is agreed that there is no direct or indirect reference to it in the Quran. However, most Muslims agree it is a pre-Islamic rite that Muhammad incorporated into his religion. The various schools of Islamic law disagree as to whether female circumcision is obligatory or just recommended (Eile 1990:1).

After having read five volumes of Muslim Hadith and nine volumes of Al-Bukhari Hadith, twice, I am personally convinced there is no legitimate Tradition of the Prophet that either legislates or recommends female circumcision. More importantly, the Quran is silent on the subject. So, then, where did such a widespread practice originate? How can it be considered obligatory for millions of Muslim women if the most authoritative Islamic texts are silent on the subject?

Brooks postulates, "Widespread mutilation seems to have originated in Stone Age central Africa and traveled north, down the Nile, into ancient Egypt. It wasn't until Arab-Muslim armies conquered Egypt in the eighth century that the practices spread out of Africa in a systematic way, parallel to the dissemination of Islam, reaching as far as Pakistan and Indonesia" (Brooks 1995:36–37).

We have scientific evidence of how ancient the practice is. "Circumcision of women was practiced in Ancient Egypt, as the evidence of female mummies from 200 BC has demonstrated" (Dareer 1983:iii). Here Muslims have only given ongoing and widespread continuity to the circumcision of females.

Islamic clerics have issued a variety of edicts and opinions on genitalia mutilation. Sheik Yousef El-Badry is quoted in *Time* magazine's "Verbatim" section as saying, "It prevents diseases like AIDS and bad smells. It makes the woman control her sexual urges" (El-Badry 1997:9).

Such modern perspectives by authoritative religious leaders ensure the perpetuation of female circumcision. In Mauritania, men are convinced it is a religious imperative to have all of their women circumcised. They say, "It is the only method of ensuring piety and fidelity" (Aram 1990:64–65).

In the Philippines, a Christian worker had an informal conversation with several Muslim girls that revealed they have no problem with circumcision. It is usually performed at birth or near the girl's fourth birthday. Older women or relatives perform the circumcision. They explained that it is just a tradition, and all girls undergo the rite. Elders assure them that this amputation reduces their sex drive and will make them more suitable for marriage. My research indicates that female circumcision is common in Thailand, Malaysia, and Indonesia, and less-widely practiced in Afghanistan, Bangladesh, India, and Pakistan.

Even Muslim women living in the West can secure the services of a doctor to perform the prohibited operation. Brooks reports, "In London in 1992, Donu Kogbara, a *Sunday Times* investigative reporter, had no trouble finding a doctor who agreed to remove her clitoris, even though the operation has been banned in Britain since the Prohibition of Female Circumcision Act was passed in 1985. The reporter simply told the Harley Street doctor, Farouk Siddique, that her fiancé was insisting she have the operation before their marriage" (Brooks 1995:37).

Mutilation Styles

The following examples will be shocking to the uninitiated, but to millions of women around the world, this is all taken for granted as members of the female sex.

Al-Nahdah, a widely read Islamic journal published in Malaysia, quoted this Tradition, which they consider to be authoritative. "When the Muslim women of Mecca moved to Madinah there was one Ummu Athiah whose work was to circumcise girls in Mecca before the Hijrah. This woman used to cut too far into the clitoris and the Prophet once said to her, 'Ummu-Athiah, do not cut too deep because if the cut is not deep the girls will be prettier and will also give more enjoyment to their husbands'" (Juned 1996:12).

Unfortunately, multitudes of Muslims blindly accept these words purportedly spoken by Muhammad. One of the major goals of amputation is simply to please one's husband. Male chauvinism seems to dominate and permeate all aspects of female circumcision.

A variety of styles of mutilation are utilized in the excision process. Dr. Saadawi documents her own experiences.

"My profession led me, at one stage, to examine patients coming from various Arab countries. Among them were

Sudanese women. I was horrified to observe that the Sudanese girl undergoes an operation for circumcision, which is ten times more cruel than that to which Egyptian girls are subjected. In Egypt it is only the clitoris which is amputated, and usually not completely. But in the Sudan, the operation consists in the complete removal of all the external genital organs. They cut off the clitoris, the two major outer lips (*labia majora*) and the two minor inner lips (*labia minora*). Then the wound is repaired. The outer opening of the vagina is the only portion left intact, not however without having ensured that, during the process of repairing, some narrowing of the opening is carried out with a few extra stitches. The result is that on the marriage night it is necessary to widen the external opening by slitting one of both ends with a sharp scalpel or razor so that the male organ can be introduced. When a Sudanese woman is divorced, the external opening is narrowed once more to ensure that she cannot have sexual relations. If she remarries, widening is done again" (Saadawi 1980:9).

Saadawi goes on to use words like cruel and horrifying to describe genitalia amputation. What Saadawi has documented is not the norm among Muslim women, whose loss is confined to the clitoris. This is little comfort for the millions of Sudanese women who have been extensively mutilated.

For many women, the sewing of the outer opening of the vagina is the most painful and degrading activity associated with circumcision. An Ethiopian woman related how her clitoris was scraped with an unclean knife and then her raw flesh was sealed with inch-long acacia thorns. On her wedding night, her husband had to use his dagger to slice his way into the jagged cicatrix that had become her genitals. She experienced great pain later as she delivered four children through a birth canal that was choking on its own scar tissue (Brooks 1995:33).

Jan Goodwin writes about a conference she attended in Cairo entitled the Development of Women in the Islamic World. There she talked to a number of African women about their experiences with infibulation, the practice of cutting away the labia and the sealing the wound to leave a small opening for urine and menstrual blood. They spoke of instances where it took a man up to forty days to effect sexual penetration. But if the husband is impatient, they said, he just used a knife. They also told of "special honeymoon centers built outside communities so that the screams of the brides will not be heard" (Goodwin 1994:335).

Girls in the villages of Yemen are told that if they do not have their genital flaps of skin cut off, this skin will grow and become like a penis. This prospect induces fear, prompting the girls to actually desire circumcision. Unfortunately they never learn the truth because they have not had occasion to meet uncircumcised women (Muhsen 1991:90–91).

Brooks documents a shocking reality she learned of in Eritrea.

"When I met her, late in 1989, Dr. Abrehet worked in a hospital whose "wards"—thatched shelters with saline drips hanging from tree branches—rambled for almost three miles through a steep-walled mountain valley. Much of her work had nothing to do with the war. Instead, it involved saving women from the worst consequences of genital mutilation. In Eritrea, girls were subjected to both clitoridectomy—the excision of the clitoris—and infibulation—the cutting away of the labia and the sealing of the wound to leave only a tiny opening for urination and menstruation. If the malnourished little girls didn't bleed to death from the procedure itself, they often died from resulting infections or debilitating anemia. In others, scar tissue trapped urine or menstrual fluid, causing pelvic infections. Women with scar-constricted birth canals suffered dangerous and agonizing childbirth. Sometimes the baby's trapped head led to fatal hemorrhage or ruptured the bladder, causing seepage of urine that made the woman smell like a latrine and poisoned her later fetuses" (Brooks 1995:34).

One young girl had such a tight circumcision that she could barely pass any blood from her menstrual cycles. She was too shy to tell her mother about the problem. The accumulated blood caused her abdomen to grow. This, with the absence of menstrual blood, caused her family to think she was pregnant. As a result, her family arranged for her to be murdered in order to save "family honor" (Dareer 1983:37).

Such is the power of shame in Muslim society. Although the young girl was totally innocent, she had been caught in a web of suspicion that led to her demise. Female circumcision was the first link in this tragic downward spiral.

Reflections

Religion and female circumcision. How is it possible for the two to intersect? Again, Dr. Saadawi's reflections are thoughtful and forceful.

"If religion comes from God, how can it order man to cut off an organ created by Him as long as that organ is not diseased or deformed? God does not create the organs of the body haphazardly without a plan. It is not possible that He should have created the clitoris in woman's body only in order that it be cut off at an early stage in life. This is a contradiction into which neither true religion nor the Creator could possibly fall. If God has created the clitoris as a sexually sensitive organ, whose sole function seems to be the procurement of sexual pleasure for women, it follows that He also considers such pleasure for women as normal and legitimate, and therefore as an integral part of mental health. The psychic and mental health of women cannot be complete if they do not experience sexual pleasure" (Saadawi 1980:42).

At this point, I must admit that there are tribal African Christian women who are circumcised and who continue to perpetuate this experience on their daughters. Even in African churches related to my mission, this traditional practice lives on, passed from generation to generation.

A few years ago, I was driving around Charlotte, North Carolina, with one of the church leaders from the Ethiopian Church related to our mission. Very carefully, I broached the subject of female circumcision with him. He responded with obvious embarrassment. "Phil, it is wrong. We are sad it continues to be practiced. And at the highest level of church administration, we are concerned. But it is an engrained cultural custom. If we come out and denounce it too strongly, we will drive people out of the church. Therefore, we are dealing with it incrementally. Hopefully, soon it will exist no more."

Yes, sad indeed. According to my research, female circumcision has never had any type of Judaic or Christian religious sanction or endorsement. That includes the entire Bible as well as that which emanates from the interpreters of our Scriptures and religious traditions. The same cannot be stated of Islam. It is much more than a tribal inheritance passed on through the generations. Today in most, and I use that word advisedly, of the Muslim world, female circumcision is a prescribed religious obligation.

The protests continue to be shrill, both within and without the Islamic world. A Westerner ponders, "Is it even our fight?

As a mental test, I always try to reverse the gender. If some ninety million little boys were having their penises amputated, would the world have acted to prevent it by now? You bet" (Brooks 195:237).

But there is a call for a broader approach to the subject, as raised by Dr. Saadawi herself.

"I am against female circumcision and other similar retrograde and cruel practices. I was the first Arab woman to denounce it publicly and to write about it in my book, *Woman and Sex*. I linked it to the other aspects of female oppression. But I disagree with those women in America and Europe who concentrate on issues such as female circumcision and depict them as proof of the unusual and barbaric oppression to which women are exposed only in African or Arab countries. I oppose all attempts to deal with such problems in isolation, or to sever their links with the general economic and social pressures to which women everywhere are exposed, and with the oppression which is the daily bread fed to the female sex in developed and developing countries, in both of which a patriarchal class system still prevails.

"Women in Europe and America may not be exposed to surgical removal of the clitoris. Nevertheless, they are victims of cultural and psychological clitoridectomy" (Saadawi 1980:xiv).

Once again, we in the West are perceived to be arrogant and aggressive. How easy to be caught up with the "speck of sawdust in your brother's (sister's) eye and pay no attention to the plank in your own eye" (Matthew 7:3). The nominally Christian West has an abysmally poor record of dealing with abortion, pornography, and female abuse. In all too many instances, the female is left with intact genitalia, but made barren with an excised soul.

It is my desire to see us lower the decibels of our protests over female circumcision. May we proceed with a graceful interaction with Muslim men and women as we make our case against a medieval practice that denigrates and dehumanizes. Yes, let it be accomplished, but with a love and humility that attracts rather than repels.

8

Sex

Sultana, a Saudi Muslim princess, comments on female sexuality in Jean Sasson's *Princess Sultana's Daughters*:

"In my country it is prohibited by religious law for single men and women to see each other. While inside the country, men socialize with men, and women with women. Since we are prevented from engaging in traditional behavior, the sexual tension between those of the same sex is palpable. Any foreigner who has lived in Saudi Arabia for any length of time becomes aware that homosexual relations are rampant within the kingdom.

"I have attended many all-female concerts and functions where quivering beauties and suggestive behavior triumph over heavy veils and black abaayas. An orderly gathering of heavily perfumed and love-starved Saudi women festers into spontaneous exuberance, bursting forth in the form of a wild party with singing of forbidden love accompanied by lusty dancing. I have watched as shy-faced women danced lewdly with other women, flesh to flesh, face-to-face. I have heard women whisper of love and plan clandestine meetings while their drivers wait patiently in the parking lots. They will later deliver these women to the husbands who are that same evening being captivated by other men" (Sasson 1994:44).

Is this an anomaly, or a regular occurrence throughout the Muslim world? In this chapter I will seek to explore at least some of the tensions regarding sexual expression that are commonly found within the *ummah* (community) of worldwide Islam.

Conservative Values

Modesty is recurrently enjoined throughout scriptures of the Islamic faith. Most of the references concern women. The common belief is that if women are properly sequestered and protected, then men will not be unduly sexually tempted.

There is precedent for Muslim women to be homebound. The wives of the Prophet were exhorted to "stay in your houses" and "be regular in prayer" (Quran 33:33). A dedicated Muslim woman strives to emulate that which was incumbent upon Muhammad's wives, especially in regard to commands from the Quran.

My close Arab Christian friend was walking down the streets of Damascus holding hands with his fiancée. Within a few minutes, Muslims approached him and informed him that he must cease his improper behavior with his soon-to-be wife. In a similar experience, when Julie and I first arrived in Dhaka, Bangladesh, in 1962, we began holding hands as we walked down the street together. We had only been married for nine months and this seemed to us to be an appropriate expression of tenderness to each other. Immediately, our senior missionary instructed us to unclasp our hands. Even such an innocent public display of affection between a husband and wife was unacceptable in this new, strange Muslim culture.

One Arab Muslim felt a sense of overwhelming shame as she watched her relative holding hands with her boyfriend. Her reaction? "I have been in the hitta [market] for twenty-five years and I have netted this shop one thousand pounds. Yet I am going to sell the shop and leave the hitta because of the disgraceful behavior of my relative" (el-Messiri 1978:533).

A Muslim man gives his perspective on his relationship with his new bride.

"We asked him whether he saw much of Fatima during the months preceding the wedding. Ali explained: 'Yes, a few times in her home. That I could do because she is my relative, but never had she been a stranger. When the two are of the same family, they should see each other, speak together, and know each other one full month before they marry, so that they will know each other's character.'

"'What about touching, or physical caresses?' I [Wikan] asked impudently. Ali recoiled at the mere thought:

"'No, no, unchastity is not practiced here! Before marriage, you should not touch her. If you asked her to do such a bad thing with you, and she consented, how could you think she should not do it again?...One must think to the future'" (Wikan 1982:248).

Many other illustrations could be given. The Islamic ideal is for absolute sexual purity to be maintained for one's wife and daughters. They are to be protected with all the force of family honor. Unfortunately this high standard is not enforced for Muslim men. Even though Islamic scriptures mandate male morality, the reality is that this standard is seldom met. Great allowance is given to men's sex drive, which allows them to go beyond that which is prescribed religiously. Many times I have asked Muslim friends how they justify their immoral behavior. Their answer? "We are weak, and Allah is merciful." There they rest their case, awaiting the Great Day of Judgment.

Promiscuity

"Madonna is a good Christian because of her name and the cross necklaces she frequently wears." If the average Christian heard such a statement, he would protest such a caricature and declare Madonna to be but a reprobate believer, if that. Herein lies the struggle in addressing this issue of promiscuity among Muslim women. Imams and devout believers would fervently deny promiscuous women are true Muslims, and I concur. But, having acceded to that argument, I would be remiss to omit a reality among Muslims that, however distasteful, is a growing phenomenon worldwide.

My first shock regarding Muslim immorality occurred when we arrived in a small village in Bangladesh in 1962. Our tin home was near the market and about one hundred yards from a cluster of bamboo shacks. I had often noticed young women dressed in colorful saris and wearing bright red lipstick standing around these houses. Within a few days, I was warned not to venture near those "ladies of the night." In complete openness, these women, living in a relatively tight Muslim society, were soliciting men. Sexual favors for rupees. Friends told me all was legal, as long as the women stayed in that area.

A further shock came when a young man began coming to our home to visit with our much older, somewhat deformed, and unattractive house helper. At first we thought that they were relatives. But soon people began to assure us of the impossible. There was a sexual affair going on between two of the most improbable people in our village. We had to dismiss our helper. To this day we ponder the reason for such a relationship.

Another incident occurred during those first five years that we spent immersed in Muslim culture. Just outside our home, we had a small, tin building that housed the Bangladesh Bible Correspondence School office. A young, handsome Christian clerk assisted us in our ministry. His desk was near the back door of the office. One day I noticed an attractive, young, married Muslim woman sitting in the entrance of her home. Her chair was positioned so she could gaze across some thirty feet into the eyes of our clerk. She frequently allowed her sari to fall off her shoulders, which made for a most sensual posture. After a rather frank discussion with our clerk, we decided to move his desk into a more secluded location in the office.

In my naiveté, I had thought that societal restraints within Muslim Bangladesh would disallow sexual promiscuity. What I discovered was that sex went underground. In our twenty years in Bangladesh, we never encountered overt pornography, X-rated movies, or even couples touching in public. But the allurements of the flesh found expression in the shadows.

A Muslim Filipino judge talked to me frankly and boastfully. He told of his frequent travels that necessitated being absent from his wife. "What am I to do? I have sexual needs. So I find an attractive young girl who is in financial distress. We have sex and two things happen: I meet her peso needs, and she provides me with sexual release. No harm in that. It is good for both of us."

No problem for him, but what if his wife had sex with a man during his absence? A scandal, beatings, a divorce, and maybe even an arranged "honor killing" would result. Double standard, indeed.

Unni Wikan, in *Behind the Veil in Arabia,* relates how

sex is a frequent point of conversation among women at parties held in Oman.

"An interesting feature of these occasions, with important effects on children's socialization, is the extent of sexual joking and chatting that goes on. Sex is a favorite topic of women. Vivid descriptions in words and gestures of manners of intercourse within and without marriage, as well as sexual aberrations of various kinds, have a prominent place in their informal gatherings. They observe no shyness for children, not even for a son in his teens. For this reason, children presumably grow up with a 'natural,' matter-of-fact attitude to these aspects of life" (Wikan 1982:85).

It would appear that a type of sublimation occurs in these social gatherings. Women talk sexually; men perform sexually. The women have a verbal catharsis that probably meets the needs of most of those present.

I conclude this section with just one illustration of lesbian experience. My research indicates this does happen, though not talked about and rarely seen. It would seem it is safe ground—not adultery, not fornication—and the secret outlet for sexual passion. Cherry Mosteshar describes one incident, which occurred in a city in Iran.

"One of my new and very dear friends had two daughters whom she guarded against the taint of romantic contact with men. At twenty-one her eldest daughter, Soosan, had never been out with a boy; she had never been to a party without her parents or her twenty-five-year-old brother—himself proud of being celibate. She had yet to be allowed to go out after dark on her own, even if it was just to the next tower block. After leaving school at seventeen, Soosan had sat at home waiting for the day she would be wed. She didn't have the talent or the inclination to go to university, nor could she work for a living in an ordinary job—this would be considered to shame her middle-class parents, who would appear as if they could not support their daughter. So she spent her days with her Mother's friend or with the daughters of a neighbour, particularly the nine-year-old daughter. It was at the home of this neighbour that I saw a sight that at first turned my stomach and then filled me with sorrow.

"While the two girls' Mothers discussed their fascinating morning of shopping with me, Soosan and the little girl sat on the floor. Slowly the elder girl put her head on the younger girl's lap and then to my horror I saw them in a deep mouth-to-mouth embrace. The kiss was passionate and I squirmed in my seat as their Mothers paid not the least bit of attention to the 'snogging'. I wanted to lash out, to tell them that they were allowing the child to be sexually abused" (Mosteshar 1996:103).

Mutah

A young Muslim Filipino looked at me and, with a touch of pride in his voice, said, "I've converted from Sunni to Shia Islam." Immediately I understood. I replied, "Oh, that means you are wanting to engage in *mutah* (temporary marriage)." Abdul looked a little like a two-year-old who had just been caught with his hand in the cookie jar. "How do you know about mutah?" he asked nervously. From there, our frank discussion revolved around his desire to legally have sex with multiple women.

The *Oxford Encyclopedia of the Modern Islamic World* gives this succinct and authoritative definition of *mutah*: "A pre-Islamic tradition, *mutah* ("temporary marriage") still has legal sanction among the Twelver Shiis, residing predominantly in Iran. It is often a private and verbal contract between a man and an unmarried woman (virgin, divorced, or widowed). The length of the marriage contract (ajal) and the amount of consideration (ajr) given to the temporary wife must be specified; temporary marriage may be contracted for one hour or ninety-nine years. The objective of *mutah* is sexual enjoyment (istimta); that of permanent marriage (*nikah*) is procreation (*tawlid-I nasl*)" (Haeri 1995:212).

Mutah is not an Islamic innovation. Rather it was an ancient pre-Islamic custom practiced by Arabian tribes. Some scholars see this as a practice that facilitated a temporary alliance between a stranger seeking protection and the tribe that provided him refuge (Haeri 1983:232). It was this custom which Muhammad adopted into his new Islamic faith.

Quranic authentication of Mutah is thin. It is based on chapter 4:24, "And those of whom ye seek content (by marrying them), give unto them their portions as a duty. And there is no sin for you in what ye do by mutual agreement after the duty (hath been done)." Shia interpreters replace "seek content" with "seek pleasure." They also add "for a specified period" into the verse (Mahdavi 1985:263).

Reliable Hadith is more explicit on Muhammad's allowance of Mutah. "While we were in an army, Allah's Apostle said, 'If a man and a woman agree (to marry temporarily), their marriage should last for three nights, and if they like to continue, they can do so; and if they want to separate, they can do so'"(7:37; 62.32.52).

Another Tradition says, "Narrated Abdullah: We used to participate in the holy wars carried on by the Prophet and we had no women (wives) with us. So we said (to the Prophet), 'Shall we castrate ourselves?' But the Prophet forbade us to do that and thenceforth he allowed us to marry a woman (temporarily) by giving her even a garment, and then he recited: 'O you who believe! Do not make unlawful the good things which Allah has made lawful for you'" (6:110; 60.107.139).

These Hadith are obviously referring to a context of men in battle, deprived of sex with their wives. But the Prophet goes on to give Quranic allowance for mutah by quoting a verse that indicates that temporary marriage falls under the category of lawful things. Since the Quran is an infallible source of doctrine and ethical behavior, Shia Muslims take this as conclusive proof that mutah is a permanent institution sanctioned by God.

The Sunni Muslim community, ninety percent of all Muslims, strongly disagrees. They point to another Hadith, "Ali said, 'Allah's Apostle forbade the mutah marriage on the Day of the battle of Khaibar'" (9:76; 86.4.91). Sunnis contend that mutah was a temporary allowance later cancelled by the Prophet. Umar, the second caliph, made a strong ruling against mutah. Sunni Muslims follow Umar while the Shia Muslim community, which mostly resides in Iran and is ten percent of all Muslims, carries on with the practice of mutah.

Men are allowed to have as many temporary wives as they desire. They draw up a contract that stipulates the length of time the two will live together. Within the agreement, the man's financial obligation to the woman is described. This contract may or may not get notarized, and witnesses are optional.

A temporary wife may have only one husband at a time. This is so that parentage can be discerned if she becomes pregnant. In such an event, the child goes to the father and takes his or her place as a legal offspring with all the rights and privileges of the man's children from his permanent marriage. The temporary wife may not remarry until two menstrual periods have passed. This also is to avoid controversy over parentage if she becomes pregnant.

So what is the distinction between mutah and prostitution? The Shia rationale is clear. "An important distinction between muta and prostitution is a religious and conceptual one: prostitution in religious thinking, represents disorder, disobedience to the established rules, corruption, and indulgence in sinful and unlawful sexual activities. It is fornication, which is explicitly condemned in the Quran. It is viewed as detrimental to the society's general health and welfare, and goes against its stated ethics and ethos. While performing a similar function, *muta* symbolizes social control and harmony with the social order. Although serving to gratify sexual needs, it is presumably not an anti-social behavior. Rather, participants are following a divinely-recommended way to gratify these needs. Significantly, not only is *muta* not considered immoral, it is perceived to combat corruption and immorality" (Haeri 1983:234).

Sadly, this view is even promoted in Iranian schools. Mutah is discussed in a contemporary religious education textbook that is geared toward students over ninth grade. The text says youth have sexual needs that can be met through temporary marriage. Permanent marriage is depicted as costly and something to be delayed until the youths have attained financial stability. In the meantime, mutah is a legitimate sexual outlet for young people (Haeri 1983:240).

Some years ago, I had a splendid opportunity to interact with Zia, an Iranian Muslim convert, about mutah. Zia said mutah is widely practiced in Iran. It is not a sin and produces no feelings of guilt. He said that Iranians talk about mutah experiences in the same way Americans talk about kissing a girl on a date. Temporary marriage is often negotiated with prostitutes. Imams are ardent practitioners of mutah. Iranians emphasize the widespread promiscuity of the West. Men often use their girlfriends for sex and discard them at whim. There is no obligation for the man, usually not even if the woman becomes pregnant. Shia Muslims point to the "gift" given to the woman in mutah: She must agree to the relationship, and the man is responsible if she becomes pregnant. As a Christian, I can only conclude that mutah is legalized prostitution with Islamic sanction. Likewise, I denounce Western promiscuity. My only consolation is that our New Testament does not give fornicators, adulterers, or live-ins religious authentication.

Sexual Violations

Iqbal, an elderly Muslim lawyer told me that a man needs a fresh spouse every ten years in order to meet his sexual needs. And true to his word, he has had six wives, three of whom he has divorced. Iqbal has operated well within Quranic parameters. Never more than four wives at a time, and he has financially cared for each one.

A father threatening incest is not uncommon. My close Bangladeshi Muslim friend, Dr. Ali, told me that in Bangladesh when a rural Muslim father gets angry with his daughter, he will tell her, in a threatening voice, to do as she is told or he will have sex with her.

Dr. Saadawi graphically illustrates sexual abuse within the family.

"The only female whom a young boy or man can probably find within easy reach is his young sister. In most homes she will be sleeping in the adjoining bed, or even by his side in the same bed. His hand will start touching her while she is asleep, or even awake. In any case it does not make much difference since, even when awake, she cannot stand up to her older brother because of fear of his authority which is consecrated by custom and law, or fear of the family, or as a result of a deep-seated feeling of guilt arising from the fact that she may be experiencing some pleasure under the touches of his hand, or because she is only a child, not able to understand exactly what is happening to her" (Saadawi 1980:14).

Such terrible happenings are not unknown in the West, but it is my considered opinion that Muslim girls are at greater risk due to societal norms that are prevalent in Islamic society. A male can easily be driven to sexually exploit an accessible female. Regrettably, it often turns out to be a sister or a cousin.

Another example of sexual abuse relates to women in prison. It has been documented that seventy-two percent of all women held in Pakistani prisons are sexually abused. Some seventy-five percent of all women in Pakistani jails are there because of charges of adultery against them. They can wait for years for their trials to be held (Goodwin 1994:52).

One wonders how many men are in Pakistani prisons on charges of adultery. After all, it does take two people to commit.

The West stands indicted as well. Terrible acts of sexual crime against women are committed. The difference is that in the West one can dial 9-1-1 and be reasonably assured of sympathetic justice. For millions of Muslim women, the opportunity to call for help is out of reach.

Societal Punishments

Princess Sultana's seventeen year-old Saudi friend was the victim of Islamic "justice." Nadia was guilty of immorality and drowned in her family's swimming pool. Princess Sultana shares her emotional reaction.

"At ten o'clock the next morning, I sat alone, staring yet unseeing out my bedroom balcony. I thought of Nadia and imagined her bound in heavy chains, dark hood gathered around her head, hands lifting her from the ground and lowering her into the blue-green waters of her family swimming pool. I closed my eyes and felt her body thrashing, her mouth gasping for air, lungs screaming for relief from the rushing water. I remembered her flashing brown eyes and her special way of lifting her chin while filling the room with laughter. I recalled the soft feel of her fair skin, and considered with a grimace the quick work of the cruel earth on such softness. I looked at my watch and saw that it was 10:10, and I felt my chest tighten with the knowledge that Nadia would laugh no more" (Sasson 1992:102).

Many Muslims would read these words and say that justice had been accomplished and family honor was restored. My reaction is an increased heartbeat, a furrowed brow, and a tenseness that courses throughout my body.

I also felt such sadness as I watched the film on CNN that was made, at great personal risk, about Afghan women. Two scenes are indelibly marked upon my soul. One was the harsh beating of a fully veiled woman whose only sin was to momentarily show her face in public. The other was that of an open pick-up truck driving into the middle of a sports stadium. A veiled woman was taken from the back of the truck and made to kneel. Then, in horrific slow motion, the film showed the bearded Muslim executioner bring his rifle to the woman's head, and with a single shot, dispatch her soul into eternity. The on-looking crowd cheered. Is it too much to speculate that perhaps God cried?

In 1972, I visited Kabul for one week. I had the privilege

to speak to a tentmakers group that had gathered in a home. What a magnificent town, ringed by majestic mountains. The atmosphere on the streets was relaxed and friendly. Afghan women wore veils, but their faces were uncovered. But just a few years later, Afghanistan began its descent into suppression and violation when fundamentalist Islam moved in.

Princess Sultana tells another story of another execution that took place in Saudi.

"When I was twelve years of age, a woman in one of the small villages not far from Riyadh had been found guilty of adultery. She was condemned to die by stoning. Omar and our neighbours' driver decided to go and view the spectacle.

"A large crowd had gathered since early morning. They were restless and waiting to see the one so wicked. Omar said that just as the crowd was becoming angry with impatience in the hot sun, a young woman of about 25 years of age was roughly pulled out of a police car. He said she was very beautiful, just the sort of woman who would defy the laws of God.

"The woman's hands were bound. Her head hung low. With an official manner, a man loudly read out her crime for the crowd to hear. A dirty rag was used to gag her mouth and a black hood was fastened around her head. She was forced to kneel. A large man, the executioner, flogged the woman upon her back; fifty blows.

"A truck appeared and rocks and stones were emptied in a large pile. The man who had read off the crime informed the crowd that the execution should begin. Omar said the group of people, mostly men, rushed toward the stones and began to hurl the rocks at the woman. The guilty one quickly slumped to the ground and her body jerked in all directions. Omar said the rocks continued to thud against her body for what seemed to be an interminable time. Every so often, the stones would quiet while a doctor would check the woman's pulse. After a period of nearly two hours, the doctor finally pronounced the woman dead and the stoning ceased" (Sasson 1992:183–184).

Obviously morality is an important component of Muslim society. The Hadith reports the Prophet as saying, "Whoever can guarantee (the chastity of) what is between his two jaw-bones and what is between his two legs (i.e., his tongue and his private parts), I guarantee Paradise for him" (VIII:320; 76; 223:481). It can be assumed that if Paradise is guaranteed for "him," the same is true for "her."

The Quran actually speaks of equal punishment for both sexes in adultery. "The adulterer and the adulteress, scourge ye each one of them (with) a hundred stripes" (Quran 24:2). Another verse from the Quran specifies what is to be done to lewd women. "As for those of your women who are guilty of lewdness, call to witness four of you against them. And if they testify (to the truth of the allegation) then confine them to the houses until death take them" (Quran 4:15).

Perhaps it can be assumed that the woman is first scourged with one hundred stripes and then placed under house arrest until she dies. The "four witnesses" who are called to testify seem to be an attempt to ensure the guilt of the accused.

A Hadith reinforces the flogging penalty. "The verdict of Allah's Apostle was sought about an unmarried slave girl guilty of illegal sexual intercourse. He replied, 'If she commits illegal sexual intercourse, then flog her (one hundred stripes), and if she commits illegal sexual intercourse (after that for the second time), then flog her (a hundred stripes), and if she commits illegal sexual intercourse (for the third time) then flog her (a hundred stripes) and sell her for even a hair rope'"

(8:548; 82.22.822).

Another issue that frequently causes punishment is an illegitimate pregnancy. In Saudi, the penalty for the birth of an illegitimate child is physical punishment. The woman is not to be whipped for two years, as that is the time allotted for breastfeeding the child. For fear of her life, the girl almost always gives her child to others to raise. After two years have passed, the mother is whipped between ninety and one hundred and fifty times. She may then keep the child, but few do because of shame (Goodwin 1994:232).

Murder frequently takes place in the Muslim world in the name of preserving family honor. Almost always, the relative-killer is either given a light jail sentence or is completely exonerated. The guilty party is the adulteress, not the murderer.

A full-page of text and pictures was published in a Riverside, California, newspaper under the headline, "Death for dishonor: Women slain for perceived wrongs." An excerpt follows:

"Nora Ahmed was on her honeymoon when her father cut off her head and paraded it down a dusty Cairo street because she had married a man of whom he did not approve.

"Begum Gadhaki was sleeping next to her 3 month-old son when her husband grabbed a gun and shot her dead. A neighbor had spotted a man who was not a family member near the field where she was working in Pakistan's Sindh Province.

"Hundreds of women like Ahmed and Gadhaki perish every year because their male relatives believe their actions have soiled the family name. They die so family honor may survive" (Abu-Nasr 2000:A-24).

There is nothing in the Quran that allows an adulterer to be stoned or killed. The Hadith, however, gives Muhammad's imprimatur to such a penalty.

"The Jews came to Allah's Apostle and told him that a man and a woman from amongst them had committed illegal sexual intercourse. Allah's Apostle said to them, 'What do you find in the Torah about the legal punishment of Ar-Rajm (stoning)?' They replied, '(But) we announce their crime and lash them.' Abdullah bin Salam said, 'You are telling a lie; Torah contains the order of Rajm: They brought and opened the Torah and one of them placed his hand on the Verse of Rajm and read the verses preceding and following it.' Abdullah bin Salam said to him, 'Lift your hand.' When he lifted his hand, the Verse of Rajm was written there. They said, 'Muhammad has told the truth; the Torah has the Verse of Rajm.' The Prophet then gave the order that both of them should be stoned to death" (Hadith 4:532–33; 56.25.829).

In another Hadith, the Prophet made a distinction between the adulterer and adulteress. "The Prophet said, 'Your son will get a hundred lashes and one year's exile.' He then addressed somebody, 'O Unais! Go to the wife of this (man) and stone her to death.' So, Unais went and stoned her to death" (3;535; 49.5.860).

As I conclude this chapter, I am pensively dreaming about the almost impossible task of bringing the Western world and the nations of Islam into some semblance of understanding and appreciation for each other. Both cultural and religious communities have strengths and weaknesses, but unfortunately these differences are often confrontative rather than complementary. As a Christian, I can only pray for persevering patience as I, a lonely voice of little consequence in worldly matters, issue a call for Christians and Muslims to seek to humanize women in a new way.

For the West, protest pornography that presents women as flesh to be devoured; honor all women as one does a mother or sister; and allow women's job opportunities and salaries to be equal with men.

For the Muslim world, condemn outrageous penalties against those who have no voice; strip away the veil that dehumanizes and makes God's creation into something anonymous and abstract; outlaw mutah and declare it to be unacceptable in Islam; and teach young men to love, nourish, protect, and honor women.

And so my dream goes on.

9

Marriage and Polygamy

Al-Ghazali, the famous Muslim theologian, mystic, and religious reformer, wrote in the eleventh century what he perceived to be the advantages of marriage. A millennium later, most Muslims still affirm this somewhat chauvinistic ideal of the marital experience.

Offspring (that is the origin, and for this marriage was instituted).

The overcoming of carnal desire (to be protected from the devil).

The organization of the household, cooking, sweeping, spreading the carpets for sleeping, cleansing the vessels, caring for livelihood.

The increase of the kinsfolk (gaining more strength by the mixing of the families to protect oneself against evil and to gain welfare/security). (Walther 1995:60)

Having children, providing sexual enjoyment, and keeping a neat house. This is the destiny of over ninety percent of all Muslim women worldwide. This, to them, is what marriage is all about. It is also a fair assessment of marriage for all races and religions down through the centuries. Only in recent times have women taken on a more public role in society. Historically there have always been exceptions, but the norm is often as presented by Al-Ghazali.

Apart from Al-Ghazali's basics, there are many distinctions within Islamic mores that regulate and bring color to Muslim marriages. These vary from country to country, but commonalities appear, regardless of ethnicity, because of the influence of the Quran and Hadith. In this chapter, I will seek to highlight some of these areas.

Requirements for Marriage

The Quran prohibits a Muslim man from marrying an idolater: "Wed not idolatresses till they believe; for lo! A believing bondwoman is better than an idolatress though she please you; and give not your daughters in marriage to idolaters till they believe, for lo! A believing slave is better than an idolater though he please you" (Quran 2:221).

Muslim men can, however, marry outside the faith. The Quran says, "The virtuous women of the believers and the virtuous women of those who received the Scriptures before you (are lawful for you) when ye give them their marriage portions and live with them in honor" (5:5). It is not uncommon for a Muslim man to marry a Christian woman, and many of them later convert to the Islamic faith.

The reverse is not true. Muslim women are not permitted to marry men who are outside of Islam. The rationale for this prohibition is that they may be pressured to convert to their husband's faith. Also there is the issue of the children. There is an expectation that the children will follow the religious practices of the father. In addition to the faith requirement is a man's desire for a beautiful wife. Al-Ghazali, though writing centuries ago, has accurately portrayed a Muslim man's fantasy. "A wife is to be beautiful, non-temperamental, with black pupils, and long hair, big eyes, white skin, and in love with her husband, looking at no one but him" (Glaser 1998:48). Change "white skin" to "light skin," and you have the contemporary view of a desirable wife. One of the first questions asked about a prospective spouse is, "Is she fair-skinned?" The lighter the skin tone, the better. This is so desirable that the bride's family can demand a higher dowry for their daughter if she has light skin.

Within Islam, the dowry is an amount that is negotiated between the bride and groom's families. Marriage is not legal without an agreed-upon dowry. It is usually a large sum of money or property that is given to the bride when the marriage contract is signed.

I have met Muslim young men who have married Christian women because of the excessive dowry demands within Islamic society. Seldom have Christian families made dowry commitments a prerequisite to marriage.

Within Muslim marriages, the dowry is set up as a guarantee of the bride's financial security and protection in the marriage. It is also an insurance against separation since there is often an agreed upon sum that the wife receives in the event of divorce.

Marital Customs

There is a great deal of variation on the subject of the minimum age at which young people can marry.

"Most Muslim countries have now sought to introduce minimum ages for marriage. In most of these countries the minimum age for marriage in the case of boys is now eighteen. For girls the minimum age is fifteen in Tunisia and Morocco, sixteen in Egypt and Pakistan, and seventeen in Jordan and Syria. However, with few exceptions, marriages contracted between parties below the minimum age are still recognized as legally valid, although in some instances they attract penal sanctions. There is, in fact, a considerable amount of case law from India and Pakistan concerned with cases where children have been contracted in marriage contrary to the express provisions of the 1929 Child Marriage Restraint Act.

"Traditional Hanafi and Shiite law allows women who have reached the age of majority (that is, puberty, which the law holds may occur from the age of nine onwards and which will be conclusively presumed to have occurred by the age of fifteen) to contract their own marriages" (Coulson and Hinchcliffe 1978:39).

The Quran is completely silent on these points, but there is the Hadith to give guidance on this subject. What did the Prophet do? As mentioned earlier, Muhammad married Aisha at age six. She was taken from playing with her dolls and placed in the Prophet's house. At age nine, the first sexual relationship took place, therein consummating and formalizing the marriage. Muhammad was in his early fifties when this union took place. No Muslim I have ever heard of or read about has denied these facts. They are indisputable. Aisha was the Prophet's favorite wife. She was eighteen when he died at sixty-two. Within the majority of Islamic nations,

Muslims have struggled with this example of child marriage when trying to formulate family laws.

Fatima Mernissi has written about her research in Morocco. She found that the ideal age for marriage is when the girl is thirteen. Only ugly girls marry later in life, and that then brings shame on the family (Mernissi 1975:54).

Endogamy, or marriage within the extended family, is common among Muslims. The preferred partner is a male's first cousin on the father's side. In some communities, cousin marriages represent forty percent of all unions. In Egypt, it is more honorable for cousins to marry, so much so that non-cousin marriages are often disguised. In one sample of Sudanese women, sixty percent had married their first cousins. (Fluehr 1994:65).

First-cousin marriage is prohibited in the United States, although it is allowed in Canada. Studies on the effects of this type of marriage appear to be inconclusive. A number of Muslims I have queried have been uncomfortable with the potential risks, but the practice continues. "Even if some genetic disadvantage in first-cousin marriage were demonstrated, probably few families would make any dramatic change, because the perceived value of such marriages is so high. Indeed, in the recent period of accelerated class formation, endogamous marriage has been reinforced as a way to keep newly acquired wealth within family control" (Fluehr 1994:67).

Is the permission of the bride-to-be required in regard to the selection of a husband? A Hadith plays out the scenario: "The Prophet said, 'A matron should not be given in marriage except after consulting her; and a virgin should not be given in marriage except after her permission.' The people asked, 'O Allah's Apostle! How can we know her permission?' He said, 'Her silence (indicates her permission)'" (7:51–52; 62.42.67).

The question that arises is how many Muslim women are prepared to refuse a marriage that has been arranged by both families? In many instances, the girl does not even meet the man prior to the marriage ceremony. Acquiescence, not protest, is the norm. I have seen this played out even in the most educated of Muslim families.

Goodwin had an interesting interaction with a married Muslim woman about the merits of arranged marriages.

"Many Muslim marriages, of course, are happy. Women frequently explained to me how love should follow the wedding, not the other way around, and how arranged marriages are so much more successful than Western ones. 'Look at you,' Shafiqa told me. 'You are unmarried, and are responsible for finding your own husband. How can you do that? How will you know whether he is good or wise, or whether he comes from the right kind of family, or will be able to support you and your children? Our parents, who are experienced in marriage, know how to select two people who will be well matched in every way.'

"'When our family arranges a marriage for us, do you realize how much investigating they do? The man can hide nothing. In the West, you marry when you are in love. Both of you are trying very hard to impress each other. Only after you live together do you discover all those unpleasant surprises. I think our way is more practical. We know what to expect from the beginning'" (Goodwin 1994:93).

There are many anecdotes that represent the other side of the coin. One Muslim man, Sheikh Ali, shares with Elizabeth Fernea a sad story about his daughter, Asma.

"Sheikh Ali's young daughter Asma, it seemed, was engaged to be married. The man was a schoolteacher, not too old, of poor but morally upright parents, of whom Sheikh Ali approved. The daughter was not too excited about marrying the man and had in fact protested, but her father had paid little attention. 'I thought it was natural, she was a good girl and loved her home, probably did not want to leave it, but it was time for her to marry, that is our custom."

On a day when Asma believed both her father and mother to be out of the house, she attempted another way to get out of marriage. Sheikh continues, "I called up the stairs, 'Asma? Asma?' But she did not answer. I thought it was strange and I went up the stairs, and opened the door and there was my beautiful Asma and she was lighting a match to herself. And as her scarf flamed, I threw my arms around her and beat out the flames and cried, 'Why? Why?'...It was because she didn't want to marry!...I said, 'My God, what have I done? What has the world done? This is not Islam.' And I said to Asma, 'Stay here, my darling, for the rest of your life, don't marry, why didn't you tell me?' And she said she did, but I wouldn't listen" (Fernea 1985:213–214).

There are problems with arranged marriages. Old men marry beautiful girls of thirteen or fourteen years of age. Young women become the third or fourth wife and end up embroiled in vicious fits of rage with senior spouses. Irresponsible fathers marry off their daughters to rich men in order to gain a share of the dowry. In many instances, the reputation of the bridegroom's family is more of a consideration for the marriage agreement than compatibility between the bride- and groom-to-be.

In its best hour, arranged marriage can be exemplary. That is, when there are gracious, sensitive, selfless parents on both sides who only desire the best for their children. Unfortunately, there is plenty of room for problems within a system that continues to be perpetuated, often without critique, throughout the Muslim world.

Marriage Ceremonies

Islamic law does not prescribe any particular marital ceremony as long as there are two witnesses present. The payment of dowry to the bride, and usually to her family, is mandatory. Often the dowry is given in two parts. The first normally consists of jewelry given to the bride at the time of the wedding, and the second is a sum of money that is given in the event of divorce or upon the death of the husband (Al Munajjed 1997:22). In current times, the bride's family usually demands the money upfront for fear it will not be given if a divorce takes place.

In arranged marriages where the bride and groom have never met, something called "the moment of the first glance" often occurs. This follows the simple ceremony of commitment, for which the bride is not usually present. Bevan Jones describes this custom.

"And now the great occasion has arrived when the two are to have a peep at each other. Custom ordains that this first glimpse shall be gained by side-long glances in a mirror, be it a cheap one whose glass gives a distorted reflection, or something elaborate in a silver frame. A fine silk shawl or net is thrown over the pair and the looking-glass is placed in a position convenient for both.

"It would be considered bold and indecorous for the bride to lift her head or to look directly at the bridegroom, so she usually covers her face with her hands, too shy to let him really see her, though she observes much through her fingers. Not infrequently the groom has to implore her repeatedly to open her eyes and let him see her face. At last the bride complies and she may consider herself fortunate if the face she sees reflected in the glass is that of an attractive young man, and not of someone very much her senior in years" (Jones 1941:86).

After this, a celebration follows. The bride and groom sit quietly and with shy decorum on a raised platform surrounded by gifts, while the invitees fill themselves with an abundance of gourmet food. In some instances, dancing takes place. Gaiety, laughter, and fun are the order of the day.

As the evening progresses, the bride and groom make their way to an adjacent bedroom. What comes next can literally be a matter of life and death. The crowd often becomes silent and restless, and a spirit of apprehension hangs in the air. Fernea describes one such moment at an Iraqi wedding.

> "He has gone to his bride, I think," said Laila. The drum roll continued and the crowd shifted uneasily, whispering and chattering to each other.

> "It's taking him a long time," cackled one old lady. "What's the matter with him, is he sick?"...

> Minutes went by and the crowd grew quieter. The drum roll continued.

> There was a loud cry within, and in a few moments the bridegroom emerged smiling. After a triumphant volley of rifle shots, the groom's friends and relatives pressed forward to shake his hand. The women surged into the

compound to congratulate the bride, who would remain in her room, and to see the bloody sheet displayed by the bride's mother and the groom's mother, incontrovertible evidence that the girl was a virgin and a worthy bride. The drums ceased.

Sherifa sighed and Laila laughed with relief...

The groom's smiles meant that indeed everything was all right; the girl was a virgin, the man and his mother were satisfied (Fernea 1969:147–148).

Proof of Virginity

But what if, Allah forbid, there was no blood? There are alternative ways to produce the evidence that would be the difference between honor and dishonor, between living and dying. "Blood alone was the mark of an intact honour [hymen] on the wedding night. The *daya* [midwife] would be there with her finger tapering into a long sharp tip at the nail which she plunged into the fine membrane. Blood poured out on to the white towel which was held high to flutter above people's heads" (Musk 1995:71).

Dr. Saadawi provides documentation of what can occur when things go wrong. "Numerous were the nights which I spent by the side of a young girl in a small country house or mud hut during my years in rural Egypt, treating a haemorrhage that had resulted from the long dirty finger nail of a *daya* cutting through the soft tissues during the process of defloration" (Saadawi 1980:29).

Geraldine Brooks tells of women who have resorted to

filling their vaginas with blood-soaked sponges or splinters of glass to compensate for lost hymens (1995:57). Another ruse is done by the groom who somehow managed to have pre-marital sex with his new wife. "He, on the wedding night, would draw blood from his nose or otherwise stain his toga to conceal from the public the failure of the virginity test" (Peters 1978:317).

In some instances a medical doctor provides proof of virginity, for a fee of course. Goodwin documents one popular practice.

"A Jordanian woman marrying for the first time, no matter what her age, must be a virgin. And if she isn't, it is a simple matter to become one again. Hymenorrhaphy, or hymen restoration, is a medical procedure offered in countries throughout the Islamic world. It takes just a few minutes, in Amman costs $300, and is done on an outpatient basis and without anesthesia. 'It is quite common in Jordan' said Dr. Efteem Azar, one of the country's leading obstetrician/ gynecologists. 'It is a very simple procedure and quickly done. Anesthesia isn't necessary because if you work with a very fine needle it is less painful than an injection of painkiller would be. Hymenorrhaphy must be done three to seven days before the wedding, because the tissue is simply pulled together and the procedure doesn't last'" (Goodwin 1994:279).

There is potentially a huge price to pay if a bride does not prove to be a virgin. "Like that poor girl from the mountains who played with her cousin when she was small, and when she got married properly she wasn't a virgin. Her in-laws were furious and disowned her. They put her on a donkey facing towards its tail, with her head shaved and her arms tied, and they took her back to her family. Her elder brother stabbed her to death because she'd dishonoured the family" (Musk 1995:29).

Once again, an "honor killing" is seen as justified.

Marital Sex

Mecca is a place of holy empowerment. There is to be no defilement of Mecca, even in the way one positions himself during sex. It would be my guess that most beds of Muslims are positioned to best accommodate this prohibition.

There are other regulations to follow: no anal sex; no intercourse during a wife's period; and no sex during the daylight hours of Ramadan, although fondling is allowed. For some Muslims, full nudity during intercourse is regarded as obscene. For others, it is impractical due to the presence of children in bed with the parents.

Fatima Mernissi, a Muslim author, has described the spiritual dimensions of the sex act.

"The coital embrace is surrounded by a ceremony which grants Allah a substantial presence in the man's mind during coitus. The coital space is religiously oriented: the couple should have their heads turned away from Mecca. The symbolism of spatial orientation expresses the antagonism between Allah and the woman. Mecca is the direction of God. During intercourse, the man is reminded that he is not in Allah's territory, hence the necessity to invoke his presence.

"It is advisable for the husband to start by invoking God's name and reciting 'Say God is one' first of all and then reciting the *Takbir* 'God is the greater' and the *Tahlil* 'There is no other divinity but God' and then say, 'In the name of God the very high and very powerful, make it a good posterity if you decide to make any come from my kidney.'

"It is suitable to pronounce without moving the lips, the following words: 'Praise to God who created men from a drop of water' [Quran Surah 25:54]" (Mernissi 1975:62–63). It is my guess that such an intense spiritual orientation during intercourse is limited to a very few dedicated Muslims. I share it here as an Islamic ideal, not a practiced reality. Full ablutions are required following the sex act for both the man and woman. This is mandatory before either can pray or touch the holy Quran. When Julie and I lived in a small town in Bangladesh, I recall hearing Muslim men at the pump taking a bath right outside our bedroom window. The noise had awakened us at three in the morning. After breakfast the next morning I asked our neighbors why they were having such a late-night bath. They looked embarrassed and mumbled some unidentifiable words of excuse. In reality, they had returned from a night out with prostitutes and were performing the prescribed cleansing.

Polygamy

There are three verses in the Quran that address polygamy.

> "Marry of the women, who seem good to you, two or three or four; and if ye fear that he cannot do justice (to so many) then one (only) or (the captives) that your right hand possesses. Thus it is more likely that ye will not do injustice." (Quran 4:3)

> "Ye will not be able to deal equally between (your) wives, however much ye wish (to do so)." (Quran 4:129)

> "And all married women (are forbidden unto you save those (captives) whom your right

hand possesses. It is a decree of Allah for you."
(Quran 4:24)

To summarize, all Muslim men may marry up to four wives. These women must be "believers of the book," which includes Muslim, Christian, and Jewish women. If justice cannot be given to multiple wives, then a man should limit himself to only one. This is mostly in regard to financial matters. Men are to treat their wives equally, but this is often not possible. Because of this Quranic verse, some Muslim scholars have come out strongly against polygamy. There is no limit to the number of captives that a man may marry, and it is of no consequence if these captives are married or not. Other than captives, Muslim men may not marry women who are already married. For Shias, mutah, or temporary marriage, is allowed.

A common rationale for polygamy is reported by Bevan Jones.

"'Man by nature and by instinct is polygamous, woman monogamous...wives in at least twenty percent cases are, through diseases or insanity, unwilling to give satisfaction to the husband...the charm and beauty of the wife at 25 are at vanishing point. Is it not therefore in fairness and justice that he should take a second or third wife?' Others contend that polygamy is as moral as monogamy and that whatever element sanctifies the sex relationship in monogamy is present in polygamy also" (Jones 1941:184).

Regarding the nature of a man and the nature of a woman, it is indisputable, to me at least, that men are more sexually driven than women. To a Muslim, this is adequate proof that polygamy is created by Allah. Why would God restrict man to something that inadequately provides for his sexual needs?

Thus Allah has given a Quranic decree allowing men to have sexual release within permissible moral boundaries. I have questioned my Muslim friends whether Allah created four times as many women as men to make this social system practically feasible. Up until now, I have never received more than a smile as an answer to my query.

Muhammad Sharif Chaudhry is convinced that there are those "people," (he didn't say Muslims) who, even if they wished, cannot remain content with one wife. He contends that polygamy "comes to their rescue and saves them from the harms of unlicensed sexual indulgences." To Chaudhry, the Quran is a moral lifesaver (Chaudhry 1991:92). J.A. Badawi sees polygamy as an alternative to immorality that is consistent with human nature (Badawi 1971:8).

What about the Prophet? He was allowed an unlimited number of wives (Quran 33:50–51). A succinct apologetic for Muhammad having twelve wives is presented by Fida Hussain, a Pakistani woman with good academic credentials. In her book, *Wives of the Prophet,* she shares her convictions.

"This attack on the sacred personality of the Holy Prophet is not because of any scandal attached to his name but for the unappreciated reason that he married helpless widows from motives of humanity and altruism, as well as political expediency. Thus it comes about that the charge of sensuality has been leveled against a person who married at the age of twenty-five an elderly lady of forty and stuck to her until her death at the age of sixty-five when he himself was nearly fifty. Up to this advanced age, the Prophet of God wedded no other wife, nor is there any insinuation even in the writings of the most hostile critics, in regard to his moral integrity throughout his life, including the lifetime of his first wife, Khadijah. The charge, accordingly boils down to this, after his fiftieth year, when he was weighed down by the care of his holy mission and the onerous duties of a rapidly expanding State, he (God forbid!) waxed sensual" (Hussain 1952:4)

Nine-year-old Aisha was not a widow. The response is that her marriage to the Prophet was of a political nature. That may be true, but no one doubts the intense sexual relationship between Muhammad and Aisha. As his favorite spouse, she received favors that the other wives did not. They were extremely jealous of her. Reliable Hadith document the internal intrigues of Muhammad's wives.

So, did Muhammad wax sensual in his sunset years? Non-Muslims throughout history have answered that question affirmatively. He has been accused of using his increasing power and prestige to indulge his lusts after the death of Khadijah (Brooks 1995:80).

Where does truth lie? Perhaps one can make a strong case for Muhammad's concern for widows and his desire to consolidate political and religious control through "convenience marriages." But it is a stretch of credulity (and a proper understanding of male libido) to overlook the multiple Traditions that point to his enjoyment of sexual relations with his wives. Overemphasizing altruism as a motive for the Prophet's many marriages is a bit beyond belief.

Islamic religious leaders point out hypocrisy in Westerners who condemn the Muslim practice of polygamy. Dr. Annie Besant, as reported by Muhammad Sharif Chaudhry, has joined Muslim men in this protest.

"There is pretended monogamy in the West but there is really a polygamy without responsibility; the mistress is cast off when the man is weary of her, and sinks gradually to be a woman of the street, for the first lover has no responsibility for her future and she is a hundred times worse off than the sheltered wife and mother in a polygamous home. When we see the thousands of miserable women who crowd the streets of Western towns during the night, we must surely feel that it does not lie within the Western mouth to reproach Islam for polygamy. It is better for woman, happier for woman, more respectable for woman, to live in polygamy, united to one man only, with the legitimate child in her arms, and surrounded with respect, than to be reduced, cast out in the streets—perhaps with an illegitimate child" (Chaudhry 1991:94).

So, after these words in defense of polygamy, just how common is the practice throughout the Islamic world? One survey in 1985, revealed that only three percent of men in Libya had taken multiple wives. The figure for Lebanon was two percent, four percent in Syria, eight percent in Jordan, eight percent in Egypt, and two percent in Algeria (Barakat 1985:42). My observations in Bangladesh during our twenty years' residence there was that very few men were polygamous. There, as elsewhere, financial concerns were paramount.

Women's Perspectives

Elizabeth Fernea records an interview with a young girl who happily shares her husband, Abdulla, with a second wife, Bassoul.

> "You wonder why Bassoul and I are happier together than the sheik's wives, don't you?" she said.
>
> I nodded.

"Everyone says," she continued, "that it is because Bassoul is a good girl and helps me. This is true. But even if she were the best-hearted girl in the village and worked harder than any servant, we would not be happy together if Abdulla were not the kind of man he is. He believes the Koran and does what it says. When he goes to Baghdad, he brings back two presents: a gold bracelet for Bassoul and one for me. When Bassoul gets money for a new abayah, he always asks me whether I need one. And he divides his nights equally between us." (Fernea 1969:170)

Overall, I conclude that polygamous marriages produce much more discord than happiness. Aisha is a prime example of how this works. One Hadith records, "Aisha said, "I used to say to him [Muhammad], 'If I could deny you the permission (to go to your other wives) I would not allow your favour to be bestowed on any other person'" (6:296; 60.23.312).

Aisha obviously was experiencing a high level of jealousy. In another famous Hadith, Aisha shockingly questions the authority of how her husband received Allah's revelation.

Narrated Aisha: I used to look down upon those ladies who had given themselves to Allah's Apostle and I used to say, "Can a lady give herself (to a man)?" But when Allah revealed:

You (O Muhammad) can postpone (the turn of) whom you will of them

(your wives), and you may receive any
of them whom you will; and there is
no blame on you if you invite one
whose turn you have set aside
(temporarily). (Quran 33:51)

I said to the Prophet, "I feel that your Lord
hastens in fulfilling your wishes and desires."
(6:295; 60.240.311)

Now that is a most earthy discourse! Muhammad was in
the habit of sleeping with his wives in turns. But then he had
a revelation from Allah that allowed him to regulate his visits
according to his own desires. Aisha takes it upon herself to
directly confront her husband. She brings the revelation
process down to the level of Allah, desiring to assist the
Prophet in fulfilling his sexual preferences. Quite a teenager!

Jan Goodwin reports a testimony of one woman's sadness
within polygamy.

"I remember a discussion with a woman whose husband
had taken a second wife when she was twenty-six and had
borne six children. 'He just moved her into our home. He
didn't tell me. One day she wasn't there, the next day she
was. After that time, I sit in the same room with them and he
hardly speaks to me, he has never come into my bed again,
and he ignores our children and favors hers. It is difficult to
get him even to buy clothes for mine.' Now ten years later,
she is delighted that her husband is taking a third wife. 'Good,'
she told me. 'Now his second wife will know what it was like
for me. She can watch, as I did, as he ignores her and spends
all his time with the new wife'" (Goodwin 1994:33).

Sometimes charms are used to cause a pregnancy that
will produce a son. Otherwise, the lack of a son will often

lead a husband to take another wife. In this instance, one young girl, Laila speaks to Elizabeth Fernea about how she and her sister sought to resolve the no brother issue. "'Of course I know my father wants a son,' Laila half hissed, half whispered, 'so Fatima and I have bought a charm from Um Khalil to put in my mother's bed so she can conceive a boy. It cost three pounds. She doesn't know, but just in case that doesn't work, we have bought another to put under my father's pillow to drive out all thoughts of a second wife'" (Fernea 1969:169).

And so ends this chapter on marriage and polygamy. The worldview and perspectives are so alien to us as Westerners and as Christians. But, I hope that both I as writer and you as reader will now be able to struggle more effectively with the huge gap between Muslim and Christian, between East and West, and between the Quran and the Bible. If so, my research, writing, and pondering will have been worthwhile.

10

Married Women

An incisive, powerful poem of sadness was written by a Muslim Pakistani married woman. Read it slowly, and ponder its contents. Feel the pathos of a hurting soul, a soul that longs for intimacy, understanding, sensitivity, and, in a word, love.

Hand in Hand
I want to walk beside you through life
And you!
Want to put a ring in my nose
To pull me along.
Intoxicated by love,
I want to love you
And you!
Want to be god
Making and breaking me.
I want to dance forever in the courtyard of your heart.
And you!
Singing songs of my helplessness

On the tambourine of my needs,
Want me to dance like a puppet.
I want to become a perfume
And permeate your body
But you! Want to hide me in your pocket.
I want to cry:
And you!
Want to make me laugh as you flick your fingers.

(Goodwin 1994: epigraph)

Are all Muslim husband-and-wife relationships so estranged? By no means. But there are currents and crosscurrents in Muslim marriages that, to the Westerner, represent an enigma of major proportions. In these next pages, I will touch upon some of the highs and lows of Muslim marriage. By the end of the chapter, it will be obvious that there are strong waves of continuity and discontinuity within the Islamic institution of marriage.

So much of the world of the Muslim woman is confined. Agnes Keith tells of having visited an ancient village among the sand dunes in the interior of Libya.

"We pass through the gate in the old city wall now and step outside, into the sunshine, into a different world. The shadowed one we have left was welcoming and friendly, but not, I knew, a world for me, only for the women of a Moslem world. That world has its own strength and power which reside in its very exclusion, its walls and closed doors, its secret thoughts and unexplored minds, its faith in old ways and in the following of ancient rites. Here the old order and its followers now survive spiritually with self-respect. Tear down the walls, open the doors, draw in the sunlight, destroy old rites and bring reason to bear on old faiths—and what would be left to them here? Where and how does Fezzan life offer them any living substitute, or alternative...

"'And are these women content to follow the old ways?' I ask.

"'Of course! They know nothing else. They accept the old tradition of complete seclusion unquestioningly, and the home is the woman's only world. She is the home; its problems and burdens are hers'" (Keith 1965:136–37).

Is the married woman "content" only because she does not know of another meaning to the word? Is she unwittingly sequestered into a prison of dingy confinement? Cut off from worldly options, can it be said that ignorance is bliss? Tradition can be safe, liberating, and fulfilling. It is what always has been.

Friendship for most married women does occur, but often not in the home with her husband. Fernea documents how it plays out among Iraqi women. She writes, "A man might be a devoted father or brother or a loving husband, but in El Nahra he was seldom, if ever, a companion. I never heard a woman discuss her emotional attitude toward her husband or her father or brother, but long hours were spent in debates about the fidelity or indifference of women friends" (Fernea 1969:155).

Another relationship of potential conflict is between the married woman and her mother-in-law, especially if they live under one roof. It was a great privilege to be an integral part of Dr. Ali's family in Bangladesh. This dedicated Muslim family has powerfully impacted my life, and I have written of them in several of my books. Ali's wife and mother have an excellent rapport with each other. Some years ago, Ali requested me to give an outsider's perspective on the sociological dynamics within the Muslim family. The forum was an academic gathering of Muslim sociologists at a conference organized by Ali. At one point in my lecture I looked over to Ali and asked a simple question, "Ali, who do you love more, your mother or your wife?" The thirty or so academics erupted in howls of laughter as Ali paused, reflected, and finally said, "I love them both equally."

Not a bad answer, but in reality, his heart response, as all the delegates knew, had to point to his mother. Ali's mother's blood courses through his veins. His first residence was her womb. She reared him with selfless love. His wife? A stranger. In his case, there was no blood relationship with her. She was an outsider until marriage. Oh, yes, a deep love has been forged between them, but there's no actual bloodline.

In many Muslim marriages, the wife is a person of convenience, a helpmate. The husband's deeper emotional ties form with his friends and, of course, with his children.

Husband's Perceptions

Muslim men have been quite vocal in pointing out the deficiencies of the female sex. This is partly explained by the ascendancy of a small women's lib group that is found throughout the Muslim world. The male is under moderate siege from these liberationists. Wahiduddin Khan goes on the offense. "Having more experience of the outside world, a man is somewhat more broad-minded than a woman. His thinking is more realistic. A woman's thinking, on the contrary, is often marked by limitations. She easily falls prey to emotion" (Khan 1995:179).

Emotionalism is the usual criticism directed against women. But other Muslim men, as documented by Yvonne Haddad, postulate that women are also intellectually inferior.

"The differences between males and females are due to (a) [a woman's] menstruation, conception, giving birth, breast feeding, staying up nights and hard work during the day. [These] lead a woman to symptoms of depression and weakness of constitution. The man is free from all this. (b) Her work at home is limited in scope and experience; it is almost routine. As for the work of the man, it is wide in scope, extensive in experience and varied in relationships, full of scheming and artfulness. This leads to a marked difference in their intellectual capacity. (c) The woman in singing lullabyes to her child does not need a powerful brain, or perfect genius; rather, she needs a kind nature and a gentle disposition. Nothing gives her more joy than to descend to the level of her child and to live with him in the scope of his world, thinking with his brain, talking in his language, playing with whatever pleases him. As for the male, he does not need affection to deal with people outside, rather he needs perseverance and strength of character, incisive intellect and initiative" (Haddad 1980:65–66).

This author sees women as needing only the brain capacity of a child. Certainly this suggestion would incur the wrath of intellectual Muslim women, at least for the segment that has any scope to protest.

Abul A'la Maududi, a Pakistani spiritual leader, now deceased, was a prolific writer. His influence among Muslims worldwide has been significant. He articulates a commonly held view among Muslim men regarding the mental and emotional deficiencies as a result of a woman's menstruation. He says, "A woman becomes emotionally cold and unstable. Sometimes she even loses the ability for reflex action; so much so that her conditioned reflexes become disordered. Due to this she begins bungling in matters of daily habit. A lady tram conductor, for instance, would issue wrong tickets and get confused while counting small change" (Maududi

1993:115).

Sultana Afroz, a Bangladeshi Muslim woman, is a close friend of Julie and me. She is highly educated, having earned a master's of arts from the John F. Kennedy School of Government at Harvard University. Her position with the Asian Development Bank centers on concerns for the large numbers of women who perish during the annual cyclone season in Bangladesh. Afroz lists the reasons she has observed for this high death rate.

- They are physically weak
- Many of them do not know how to swim
- Women have long hair
- Traditional dress of women—Sari is an obstacle
- They are poor and illiterate
- They are fatalistic in attitude
- They do not want to leave their house
- They lack power to take [make] a decision at the critical moment in the absence of men
- They have no voice in disaster management activities
- They have no knowledge of a broad range of coping mechanisms
- They do not understand a warning signal, unless it is broadcast in a local dialect and in a simple way. (Afroz 1999:11–12)

Having lived in Bangladesh for twenty years, I can affirm the accuracy of many of these points. Most of these inadequacies can be tempered or removed through an extensive education program for these women who live in vulnerable coastal areas.

The Ideal Wife

Admittedly, the definition of the ideal wife will vary from country to country and even from person to person, but there are some commonalities. Even the extremes noted here have an impact on men's thinking.

Mufti Muhammed Abdul Ghani reports on two Traditions that are frequently quoted by Muslim men. These are not authoritative, but they have certainly become well known.

> The Holy Prophet (sal-am) had said if prostration before anyone except Allah were permissible he would have ordered prostration of women before their husbands. If man orders the woman to lift a mountain she should be ready to lift it—Masnad Ahmed.

> A report in the Traditions says that if the woman licks blood and pus from the wounds of her man even then she would not accomplish her duty in full—Kanzull-Aamal. (Ghani 1981:50)

To the Westerner, the words about blood and pus sound crude, but to the Muslim this is just an appropriate way to make the point that the worth of a woman is far below that of a man.

"A meek and quiet spirit" is a biblical ideal for women within most Christian circles. In Muslim society, a "quiet and soft-spoken" woman is considered to be praiseworthy. "It must be admitted that it is the duty of the wife to welcome the husband, returning home from the outside world, with a smiling face. The bewitching smile of the wife has been endowed with that wonderful power of refreshing the husband fatigued with the day's work and injured by the unkind world outside the haven of home" (Nadvi 1982:172).

Most Western women would find this exhortation laughable. An obsequious posture before one's husband will only cause him to make more demands, says the modern married woman, who is a product of Western culture. And thus the great divide between Muslims and non-Muslims remains.

Bodily hygiene is an important part of a married woman's life, particularly in the case of being pure for ritual prayers. In Bangladesh, Julie and I were visiting the home of very devout Muslims. At the time of afternoon prayer, everyone excused themselves to go into the next room to pray, everyone, that is, except the teenage daughter of our host. We questioned her as to why she was neglecting mandatory Islamic prayer. Shyly, she looked down toward her feet and explained to us that she could not pray as she had polish on her toenails—an act which negates her prayers to Allah.

There are strict regulations regarding what is to happen when a married woman leaves her home. Though the following is a conservative view, millions of Muslim women follow it. Ibn Warraq has reinforced his points with Quranic and Hadith proof texts.

She may leave only in case of a real need.

The exit must be authorized by her husband or legal guardian.

She must be well-covered, including her face, to

avoid tempting any men who might be around; she must move with her head bowed down looking neither left nor right. (Quran 24:31)

She must not put on perfume. The Prophet has said: "Any woman who puts on perfume and passes in front of men is a fornicator."

She must not walk in the middle of the road among men. The Prophet on noticing the confusion on leaving a mosque, said: "You women do not have the right to walk amongst men—stick to the sides." She must walk in a chaste and modest manner. (Quran 24:31)

When talking to a stranger, her voice must remain normal. (Quran 33:32)

If inside a shop or an office, she must avoid being left alone behind a closed door with a man. The Prophet has said: "There can never be a tête-à-tête between a man and a woman without the devil interfering and doing his worst."

She must never shake the hand of a man. (Warraq 1995:317)

These nine points describe what most Muslim men would call the "ideal wife." Muslim men in various contexts would add to or delete from this section. Urban lifestyle varies considerably from rural, but, overall, this presents the type of wife appreciated by a multitude of Muslim husbands.

Beatings

Geraldine Brooks gives a good overview of the intense controversy surrounding the Quranic verse (4:34), which legitimizes the physical beating of a rebellious wife. "For Muslim feminists, few issues are more sensitive. 'Good women are the obedient,' says the Koran. 'As for those from whom ye fear rebellion, admonish them and banish them to beds apart, and scourge them.' Muslim feminists argue that 'scourge' is only one of the possible translations for the word used in the Koran, dharaba. They say the word can also be translated as 'strike with a feather.' In the context of the Koran, which elsewhere urges gentle treatment of women, they argue, it is illogical to accept that the word is being used in its severest definition. The passage, they say, is meant to be read as a series of steps: first, admonish them; if that fails, withdraw sex; as a last resort, hit them lightly. No Muslim emulating Muhammad would ever go as far as the third step. While the prophet is known to have deprived his wives of sex as a punishment, there is no evidence that he ever raised a hand against them" (Brooks 1995:193).

Jamal A. Badawi states, "Under no circumstance does the Quran encourage, allow, or condone family violence or physical abuse." He goes on to say there may be instances when it is appropriate "for a husband to administer a gentle pat to his wife that causes no physical harm to the body nor leaves any sort of mark" (Badawi 1995:25).

Muhammad Sharif Chaudhry speaks of the Prophet prescribing "mild punishment with a tooth stick but never with a whip. Punishment should not be excessive to injure the wife and it should not at all be inflicted on her face" (Chaudhry 1991:15). Abul A'la Maudoodi approves of using a "blow" that is not severe and not too painful. He adds the restriction that no filthy language should be used when striking one's wife (Maudoodi 1983:25–26).

Fida Hussain gives her perspective in Wives of the Prophet. She says, "As regards the right of man to chastise woman, modern opinion may take exception to it, but a careful examination of some of the extreme cases of perversion will show that it is more humane to correct, rather than to divorce and throw her on the street. The Qur'an is careful in using the word 'admonish' first and then the word 'beat'. Now-a-days women being more intelligent and educated than in ancient days, admonishing may be enough" (Hussain 1952:28).

According to one report, one in three women in the world has been battered by a man at some time. In a British study of family violence, it was found that women married to Muslim men were eight times more likely to be killed by their spouses than any other women in Britain (Brooks 1995:231).

Toujan Faisal was a forty-one-year-old television host in Jordan. She moderated a chat show that dealt with women's issues. One of her programs condemned the high rate of wife beatings that were taking place throughout the country. She received hundreds of letters from angry men who insisted that beating their wives is a God-given right (Brooks 1995:193).

Muhammad al-Qadir says that "women like difficult men who can break their will by their own will. Even though they scream, in their heart of hearts they feel the pleasure of their weakness against the strength of their men" (Hamdun 1995:102).

Qawl-ul-Haq Publications, in their book Women in Islam

quote Sayyed Qotb, a modern scholar and commentator, who justifies the beating of certain types of women. "The facts of life, and the psychological observations of certain forms of deviations indicate that this approach (beating the wife) is the most appropriate one to satisfy a particular form of deviation, reforming the behaviour of the person...and gratifying her...at the same time!" (Qawl-ul-Haq 1991:18–19)

Sawsan el Messiri contends that the husband who does not control his home and wife is not respected. He is not considered a real man, for his wife overrules him. Further, she states that "Cairo women are of the opinion that a beating is nothing but an expression of jealousy that springs from love, and they appear not to mind greatly their husbands' beatings" (el Messiri 1978:538).

As a husband who has never touched his wife in anger in over four decades of blissful marriage, I find these ideas repugnant. Though the Old Testament metes out harsh punishments for wrongdoers, never does the Bible condone wife beating. The Quran can make no such claim.

In 1993 I attended a symposium at Yale Law School entitled Islam in Modern Times. Both fundamentalist and liberal Muslim scholars presented their views in dogmatic fashion. The discussion time was animated. The Quranic sanction of wife beating took center stage as fundamentalists defended the practice and liberals sought to explain away the verse that allows it. There were no cross-aisle converts, just lots of heat and not much light.

Bill Musk, my favorite author on Islamic studies, explores this subject, ending with a penetrating autobiographical note.

"Westerners who live among Middle Easterners behold very clearly the faults of male-oriented societies. I remember my blood boiling when I first saw a Turkish male beating a female relative in a field during harvesting. I wanted to stop the world and make everything right for the girl. Experience eventually helps one to hesitate: into what image would I change 'everything' to make it all right for the female? Deep down, as my anger erupted, I held unspoken assumptions about equality, love, rights and freedom which came from my own cultural background. Perhaps some of those assumptions more closely approximated the biblical norm than did the Turkish lad's, but my own society was just as 'failing' in other terms. At least the Turkish girl knew to which family she belonged; she lived with her own father and male relatives. I and my brother and sisters were all products of a broken-down, Western culture. All four of us were adopted, rescued by our adoptive parents into a caring family from four disintegrated relationships. Who was I to judge?" (Musk 1995: 38–39)

Married Women in the Marketplace

> And covet not the thing in which Allah hath made some of you excel others. Unto men a fortune from that which they have earned, and unto women a fortune from that which they have earned. (Quran 4:32)

There is no decree in Islam that forbids married women from seeking employment when it is necessary. As I have written earlier, the preferred place for a wife is in the home rearing children. But this Quranic verse speaks of women earning "a fortune." It does not command such an activity, but it does allow for it. Even Muhammad's wife Khadija had her camel caravan. In contemporary times, the preferred professions for women are nursing, medicine, teaching, social work, and clerical employment (if these jobs can be carried out in a protected environment).

In 1998 in Bangladesh, I had a discussion with a bank manager about the proliferation of women working in almost every profession, from farming to the presidency. He thought that this was an excellent development. Now half of the population can make a great contribution to the economics of society. I asked him about the vocal opposition of the fundamentalists who decried seeing women out on the streets and in the offices. He answered, "They are a minority voice of no consequence."

Egyptian married women are among the most liberated. As Brooks reports, "In Egypt women are everywhere in the work force; in the fields, as they always have been, sowing and planting; and sitting on city sidewalks, selling their produce. But they are also in positions that would have been unthinkable in the first half of the century, when only the poorest and most wretched families subjected their women to the 'indignity' of work outside the home. Egyptian women are doctors, filmmakers, politicians, economists, academics, engineers. Mostly they are public servants, cogs in the country's bloated bureaucracy. Now, it is almost unthinkable that a young Egyptian woman won't go to work, at least until she marries. Often she will find the man she will marry among her coworkers" (Brooks 1995:178).

Egyptian fundamentalists are angry about the liberal tendencies and un-Islamic activities that go on in their country. Extreme violence, including the assassination of President Sadat, has been their response. If this segment of the population ever gains political control, it can be assumed that women will be forced to go under the veil and be consigned to a sequestered existence in their homes.

The only sector in Saudi Arabia where married women work in close proximity to men is with the Arab American Oil Company (ARAMCO) in the Eastern province. Within the huge compound, Saudi women can even drive their own cars. In the late 1960's, King Faisal issued permission for women to be employed there, but only after parents give their consent (Al Munajjed 1997:92).

A Muslim Arab contended that men do not like strong women. If a woman takes on a man's work, then she is degrading herself. "What's the point of a masculine woman? It would be as if a man were married to another man. A woman has to be fine and weak. No man likes a he-she" (Zuhur 192:99–100).

Maududi addresses this subject in his usual blunt form. He writes, "And since in the sexual life man has been made active and woman passive, she has been endowed with those very qualities alone which help and prepare her for the passive role in life only. That is why she is tender and plastic instead of rough and rigid. That is why she is soft and pliable, submissive and impressionable, yielding and timid by nature" (Maududi 1993:120).

All of these concerns take on a full-blown controversy when it comes to a woman assuming political leadership over men. Pakistan, Bangladesh, and Indonesia, the three largest Islamic populated countries in the world, have all had (or have) Muslim women presidents (or prime ministers). Benazir Bhutto broke through the glass ceiling of Islam in 1988. "When Benazir Bhutto became Prime Minister of Pakistan after winning the elections of 16 November 1988, all who monopolized the right to speak in the name of Islam, and especially Nawaz Sharif, the leader of the then Opposition, the IDA (Islamic Democratic Alliance), raised the cry of blasphemy: 'Never—horrors!—has a Muslim state been governed by a woman!' Invoking Islamic tradition, they decried this event as 'against nature'" (Mernissi 1993:1).

There is an authoritative Hadith that authenticates this concern regarding women in high political positions.

> When the Prophet heard the news that the people of Persia had made the daughter of Khosrau their Queen (ruler), he said, "Never will succeed such a nation as makes a woman their ruler" (9:171; 88.18.219).

These are the very words of Muhammad as researched by Al-Bukhari. Their reliability is seemingly beyond question. The Prophet opposed female leadership over a nation. But still there is disagreement.

"The Quran has not prohibited the rule of woman anywhere. Not to speak of prohibiting or condemning it in clear-cut words in the direct manner, the Quran has not even uttered a single word in disapproving or disfavouring it. Had it been unlawful or haram (forbidden), as the orthodox say, there would have been certainly revealed a verse declaring it so. When the Quran has not overlooked even minor issues while laying down the rules and regulations governing the conduct of an individual in the family and society, how could it overlook such an important and vital issue like the rule of woman if it is haram and adversely affects the progress and welfare of humanity. The silence of Quran on this crucial issue means that the Muslim community has been left to decide it according to the circumstances and according to their best interest" (Chaudhry 1991:170).

Thus far, the three countries where Muslim women have

been elected as ruler have had one thing in common. In all three instances, the woman had been the wife or daughter of a very popular previous ruler who died. The family name is the magic that propelled them to power. Honor has been bestowed upon the family by the masses.

Examining the world of the Muslim married woman seems to be a study in contrast, change, continuity, and, in many instances, confusion. Where do we go from here? One thing is for sure; there will be no lack of controversy surrounding the lives of over 600 million Muslim women. As to how it all plays out? Stay tuned.

11

Mothers and Their Children

To begin at the beginning, let me start with the subject of birth control. Islam is the fastest growing religion in the world. There is a good reason for this phenomenon. There are conversions to Islam, yes, but that has a minor impact on growth. Biological reproduction, having lots of children, is causing the Muslim population to swell. This activity is strongly supported by all Muslim clerics. It is only political leaders who are seeking to curtail population growth due to economic considerations.

Therefore, it is not surprising that birth control has become a debated topic within Muslim society. It is important to state that there is no direct reference to this subject in the Quran. Muhammad Abdul-Rauf comments.

"We may say that the practice of birth control, apart from the surgical sterilization method, is permissible, though undesirable, subject to certain conditions. Both parties, husband and wife, should mutually agree to it. Moreover, the method they adopt should not entail physical or psychological damage to either party. In addition, their intention should be legitimate. In short, the practice of birth control may be tolerated in special circumstances, depending on the private conditions of a couple and their intention; but it should not be made the general policy of a Muslim society" (Abdul-Rauf 1977:125).

There have been discussions taking place as to which form of birth control is more acceptable to Allah. An IUD is prohibited because it is seen as an abortifacient rather than a contraceptive. The pill can have side effects, and it may have a harmful health impact on the user over the long term. "Morning after" pills are unacceptable because they kill the embryo. Few use the rhythm method of birth control due to its unreliability. That leaves barrier methods (cap, sheath, condom) as the preferred prophylactics. Coitus interruptus is also sanctioned, though it is not regarded as sexually fulfilling for the male (Khattab 1993:57).

Most Muslims regard abortion as murder. Most imams are united in prohibiting abortion except in cases when the mother's health is endangered. In Tunisia and Somalia, despite the fact that both are Islamic countries, abortion is a legal means of combating high population (Saadawi 1980:64).

In contrast to the problem of becoming pregnant with an unwanted child is the devastation a Muslim woman faces if she discovers that she is unable to conceive. Vivienne Stacey interviewed a Christian midwife who shared the steps Afghan women take if they find they are barren.

"If, as the months pass, no sign of pregnancy appears, she will be taken to the local midwife who may give advice on special herbal potions to drink. If this is not effective, she will visit the local holy man. Some verse of the Quran will be chanted and blown on her, or a charm given her to be worn on her person—a small metal box sewn into cloth, holding pieces of paper on which verses from the Quran have been written. As a last resort, she will visit a local shrine, walking round it a certain number of times, picking up stones and putting them to her forehead, or even kissing the shrine. Afterwards, a piece of cloth is tied nearby or a nail hammered into a tree.... The childless wife is a sad person who constantly fears the threat of another wife coming into the home. The stigma of having no children is strong. Other women may feel that she is judged of God, or has the 'evil eye'" (Stacey 1995:21–22).

It is not uncommon for women to become pregnant at a young age. The following Hadith, however, certainly must be unique, even in Muslim circles. This Tradition is amplified by the translator's note, as he attempts to offer a biological explanation on how this could take place.

> Al Hasan bin Salih said, "I saw a neighbour of mine who became a grandmother at the age of twenty-one." [Translator's Note: This woman attained puberty at the age of nine and married to give birth to a daughter at ten; the daughter had the same experience]. (3:514; 48.18.831)

Boys and Girls

In Arab pre-Islamic times, the Bedouins of the desert practiced female infanticide. There was even a proverb that said that to bury a daughter was not only a meritorious act, but also a generous one, since there would be one less mouth to feed. As well, there was a fear that if the daughters grew up, there would be the possibility of their being captured and violated by their enemies (Jones 1941:14,15).

When Muhammad came on the scene, he was horrified by what he saw. Therefore, through him, came a revelation from Allah that is obscure, but Muslims contend that it prohibits one from burying young female children alive. "And when the girl-child that was buried alive is asked for what sin she was slain" (Quran 81:8–9). That is the full extent of the quote, fragmentary though it seems.

Sadly, this verse has not changed Muslim attitudes concerning the overwhelming superiority of male children over female children. This prejudice is deeply embedded in the societal norms of the Islamic world. Probably a Muslim people group does not exist that does not favor male children.

There are instances where this bias leads to terrible tragedy. Goodwin relates how she tracked down Bilquis Edhi, who oversees centers for unwanted babies in Karachi, Pakistan.

"Edhi comments, "More than five hundred babies are found every year in Karachi, in the gutters, the trash bins, on the sidewalks. The police bring them to us. Ninety-nine percent of them are girls—considered a burden in this society. A few babies are deformed. A few are boys. They are anywhere from a couple of hours old to several months. They are strangled, or suffocated with plastic, or just left to die. Dead boy babies are normally the children of unmarried mothers. If the mother is not married, she is usually killed by the men in her family.'

"In an effort to stop such murders, Bilquis started a program three years ago encouraging families to turn unwanted children over to their foundation. Outside every Edhi center hangs a metal crib with a sign that reads, 'Do not kill the innocent baby. Do not make the first sin worse.' Rare is the morning when the cribs are empty. Since the program began, and despite there being no tradition in Pakistan for adoption, the foundation has been able to find homes for seven thousand unwanted infants. Those it cannot place, it keeps in its own centers" (Goodwin 1994:66–67).

One of the saddest statements by Bilquis is that ninety-nine percent of these dead babies are girls. It is likely that the cribs are likewise filled with female babies. Oh the "curse" of being born a girl in much of the Muslim world.

This problem has become more prevalent with the availability of ultra-sound machines. The sex of the baby can be determined early on. If the child is found to be a girl, a covert trip to the back-alley abortionist can be arranged. It is not only Islam that struggles with this issue. India has sought to regulate the use of ultra-sound for expectant mothers. Too many Hindu women, under pressure from their family, were aborting female babies.

Prejudice takes many forms. In Egypt, a midwife charges twice as much for delivering a boy as a girl. The fee for circumcision is fifty percent more for boys than for girls (Glaser 1998:60). Bill Musk had a daughter born in a private clinic in Egypt on an island in the Nile. He tells of his experience.

"Various Arabs from the Gulf brought their wives to the same clinic for childbirth. Above the door in the waiting room outside the delivery suite were two naked light bulbs. I asked what was the significance of the contrasting colours: green and red. I was told that if a girl was born the red bulb was turned on; if a boy, the green one. At a red light, the waiting husband walks away upset, at a green light he is extravagant in his joy" (Musk 1995:28).

Samuel Zwemer, writing in 1915, states, "The more Moslem a country is, the greater is the degradation and the inferiority of the female sex" (Zwemer 1915:84–85). Iran, Afghanistan, Saudi Arabia, Yemen, and Pakistan are countries that would seem to prove this thesis. Other non-fundamentalist Muslim nations such as Indonesia, Malaysia, Bangladesh, Jordan, and Turkey are examples where women are accorded greater rights and freedoms.

Brooks addresses the issue of Muhammad and his multiple daughters.

"It astonished me that Muslims, who put such store on emulation of their prophet, didn't wish to emulate him in something so fundamental as fathering daughters. Muhammad is thought to have had three or four sons, two or three by Khadija and one by an Egyptian [Coptic Christian] concubine named Mary. None survived infancy. Instead the prophet raised four daughters, one of whom, Fatima, he extolled as a perfect human being. 'Fatima,' he said, 'is part of me. Whoever hurts her hurts me, and whoever hurts me has hurt God.' Fatima was the only one of his children to outlive him" (Brooks 1995:67–68).

Fatima is the second most revered female name among Muslims, after Aisha. These two women have more namesakes than any other woman since the seventh century. But a female's name is seldom used. As soon as a woman is married and bears a son, she is only known as "Mother of (her son's name)." Her identity is merged with her offspring. We have only one child, a daughter. Julie, in Bangladesh, was always referred to as "Lyndi-er Ma," that is, "Mother of Lyndi." This was a step down from having a son. Our Muslim friends would always ask us when we would have another child. We would answer, "Whenever it is the will of Allah." They smiled, knowing the propensity of foreigners to have small, planned families.

Dr. Saadawi shares an early recollection of what it means to be a young girl in an Islamic society.

"The first aggression experienced by the female child in society is the feeling that people do not welcome her coming into the world. In some families, and especially in rural areas, this 'coldness' may go even further, and become an atmosphere of depression and sadness, or even lead to the punishment of the mother with insults or blows or even divorce. As a child, I saw one of my paternal aunts being submitted to resounding slaps on her face because she had given birth to a third daughter rather than a male child, and I overheard her husband threatening her with divorce if she ever gave birth to a female child again instead of giving him a son. The father so hated this child that he used to insult his wife if she used to care for her, or even just feed her sufficiently. The baby died before she had completed forty days of her life, and I do not know whether she died of neglect, or whether the mother smothered her to death in order to 'have peace and give peace,' as we say in our country" (Saadawi 1980:12).

"To have peace and give peace." What a rationale for causing your baby girl to die. How powerful are the influence and actions of a cruel husband. Insults, blows, slaps, and the threat of a devastating divorce; these are intimidation tactics that would cower even the strongest of women.

Paul Vieille has documented what Julie and I repeatedly observed in Bangladesh. His observation was of Iranian parents and children. He writes, "At birth, the little girl is 'bitter' and her first smiles mean, 'Do not throw me out, I will find my place.' The little boy whose 'mood is bad' is better cared for, better nourished, and better dressed; people are more attentive to his needs and they find that he is easier to bring up; they accept joyfully the trouble he provokes, but take badly that given by the little girl" (Vieille 1978:453).

Some years ago, we were in the home of some close Muslim friends. There were four generations of family present. The center of attention was a four-year-old boy named Syed. He was a brat, spoiled and pampered beyond all reason. At one point he repeatedly kicked his seventy-five-year-old great-grandmother. All smiled. Armed with my Western worldview, I spoke with alarm, "Please restrain Syed! He will break her bones. They are fragile at her advanced age." Everyone smiled. The King was on his throne.

Princess Sultana of Saudi Arabia writes of the fear that gripped the household into which she was born. She says, "My first vivid memory is one of violence. When I was four years old, I was slapped across the face by my usually gentle mother. Why? I had imitated my father in his prayers. Instead of praying to Makkah, I prayed to my six-year-old brother, Ali. I thought he was a god. How was I to know he was not? Thirty-two years later, I remember the sting of that slap and the beginning of questions in my mind: If my brother was not a god, why was he treated like one?" (Sasson 1992:19)

The six-year-old Ali grew up to be a terribly immoral person. His life was degenerate in every sense of the word. Never had he known discipline in his life. Sultana had perceived Ali's power early in life.

Mazhar Ul Haq Khan reports on how women and girls in Pakistan are given inferior food and clothes. "The same discrimination is found in respect to food. The girls and women in the Purdah family always get poorer foods than their brothers, fathers and husbands. The males are served in a better and more sumptuous manner than the females, whose food is often the leftovers of the meals served to the male members of the house. The same distinction is found in clothing and shoes" (Khan 1972:76).

Princess Sultana pensively lets her mind wander into philosophical areas surrounding some of the most important events in women's lives. Does a female in Saudi Arabia even exist? Is she not a non-entity?

"The history of our women is buried behind the black veil of secrecy. Neither our births nor our deaths are made official in any public record. Although births of male children are documented in family or tribal records, none are maintained anywhere for females. Although hospital births and government record keeping are increasing, the majority of rural births take place at home. No country census is maintained by the government of Saudi Arabia.

"I have often asked myself, does this mean that we women of the desert do not exist, if our coming and our passing goes unrecorded? If no one knows of my existence, does that mean I do not exist?" (Sasson 1992:23)

Is all so bleak? Can one find any silver lining in the lives of Muslim mothers and their daughters? This chapter has documented a number of sad experiences. These would certainly be typical of millions of Muslim mothers.

But there is the other side. Millions of Muslim mothers are loved and respected by husbands and children. It is a joy to watch our friend Dr. Ali frequently go up to his elderly mother and surround her with his arms of love and honor. Muslim domestic life at its best!

Elizabeth Fernea recorded this conversation with Iraqi women.

> "And is it true," asked Basima, "that in America they put all the old women in houses by themselves, away from their families?"

I admitted that this was sometimes true and tried to explain, but my words were drowned in the general murmur of disapproval.

"What a terrible place that must be!"

"How awful!"

"And their children let them go?"

"Thank God we live in El Nahra, where the men are not so cruel!"
It had never occurred to me before, but the idea of old people's homes must have been particularly reprehensible to these women whose world lay within the family unit and whose whole lives of toil and childbearing were rewarded in old age, when they enjoyed repose and respect as members of their children's households. (Fernea 1969:185)

And on that high note, I conclude this chapter, which documents the converging streams of everyday life of Muslim mothers and their children—streams of sorrow, fear, and violence, along with the joys of honor, love, and respect.

12

Divorce

Having just arrived in Bangladesh, I was emotionally unable to process what was playing out before my eyes. I experienced shock and disbelief. Just outside our home, a young woman was hysterically holding onto her husband's waist as he pulled her along the dusty road. The Muslim man was screaming curses at her, while seeking to dislodge her vise-like grip on his body. Dogs barked. People gaped. No one made a move to assist the distraught woman.

Just nine months earlier, I had committed to love, cherish, and protect my wife until death do us part. How, I wondered, could marriage deteriorate to what I was seeing played out before me? Commitment had changed to estrangement. Later I heard the husband had uttered the horrid words of abandonment, "I divorce you." In desperation, the wife was pleading for her future, her honor, her very life.

In seeking to understand Muslim divorce, it is helpful to review pre-Islamic customs and practices. Bevan Jones elaborates on this.

"The more usual and direct mode of divorce was *talaq*. Having purchased his wife, a man's power of divorce was absolute and he could discharge his total obligation to her by paying up any remaining portion of the *mahr*, due on her, to her father or guardian. This done, he would dismiss her by pronouncing the formula, *alia taliq*, 'thou art dismissed.' He was not required or expected to furnish any reason for his action. He might show his determination to get rid of her by repeating this formula three times, either at one and the same time, or with an interval between each pronouncement. Until the third pronouncement the woman was still the husband's property, and he had more right to her than any one else.

"Yet, if a man chose, he could revoke the divorce and resume marital connection. Sometimes a man would pronounce the formula over his wife ten times and yet take her back, and again divorce her and again take her" (Jones 1941:28).

From this historical overview, one can better understand how Islam borrowed and modified existing cultural norms in regard to divorce. The husband owned his wife, the divorce initiative was his, the dowry was part of the marital agreement, and the thrice-repeated formula was a part of the divorce procedure.

Shireen Nadvi, a Muslim author, has studied how Islam was able to introduce laws that have made divorce a more humane act. "In this state of pitch darkness, the dazzling sun that was Islam made its appearance and illuminated the world. And in the wake of its all-pervading reforms in other spheres of life, the Islamic law of Divorce was revealed, abandoning all extremist practices, showed the middle course of temperance and relieved those groaning under oppression and tyranny" (Nadvi 1982:185).

Many Muslim women who are victims of divorce may not be too eager to embrace the concept that they were once in pitch darkness and now are abiding in the dazzling sun, which is illuminating their lives. Divorce is ugly, demeaning, ego destroying, and in every sense, dishonorable. Julie and I have just walked through the process with a close Muslim female friend. There was devastation on all sides. Husband, wife, child, nuclear and extended family, and friends—they all walked through a valley of tears and excruciating pain.

So what is the difference between Muslim and Christian divorce? They are both destructive, but allowed by their respective Scriptures. In the following pages, I will seek to explore the various facets of Muslim divorce. We can then try to form some conclusions as to how the two are similar or dissimilar.

The Quran sets forth some guidelines: "Expel them not from their houses nor let them go forth unless they commit open immorality" (Quran 65:1).

Another passage points to arbitration as a means to reduce the divorce rate among Muslims. "And if he fear a breach between them twain (the man and wife), appoint an arbiter from his folk and an arbiter from her folk" (Quran 4:35).

I am not at all sure this verse is followed in most divorces. The norm is that the husband makes his move unilaterally, without family and community intervention, but there are exceptions. If all else fails and divorce takes place, the couple involved can, according to the Quran, be assured of the blessings of Allah. "But if they separate, Allah will compensate each out of His abundance" (Quran 4:130).

Male Initiative in Divorce

Divorce laws vary from country to country. V.R. and L. Bevan Jones give an overview from their perspective of having lived in India for many years.

"The conditions considered essential for the validity of divorce tend to emphasize the greater power of the husband. These according to Sunni law are that, the husband must have attained his majority; he must be sane; any pronouncement of *talaq* is effective, whether declared in equivocal language, under compulsion, or in jest; no witnesses are required; the pronouncement need not be made in the presence of the wife. Shi'a law, on the other hand, demands that there shall be intention to dissolve the marriage and requires the presence of two reliable witnesses" (Jones 1941:150).

In any event, the simple statement, "I divorce you," is uttered three times by the husband. This seems to be a carry-over from pre-Islamic days. The issues of witnesses, legal documents, the return of the dowry, and how long it takes for divorces to be legally finalized have been the subject of numerous religious and secular legislation throughout the Muslim world. It is interesting to note that a majority of Muslim countries have legal systems that have more in common with their former colonial rulers than with Islamic Shariah law. And that after fifty years of independence!

The divorce "formula" can be a tool of devastating intimidation. "Arab men have coined an easy, threatening phrase 'Alia Talak' (I would swear to divorce you) which they use as a prefix to every order they issue to their wives. In consequence, many Arab women live under the daily threat of being divorced" (Shaaban 1988:131).

A lecturer in Kuwait gave his insight as to how the Muslim male has a God-given authority over divorce procedures.

"'Marriage,' announced Dr. Muhammad in ringing tones. 'Marriage is half of religion. Marriage is sacred.' He sipped from a glass of water on the speakers' podium.

"'God,' he continued, 'God has given man authority over marriage, since He understands the importance of marriage, and the necessity of a strong and reasonable guardian of that institution. God has therefore also given men authority over divorce, that splitting of the sacred bond. Why has God given men authority over divorce?' Dr. Muhammad took another sip of water. 'Because men are more rational than women. Thus men will make the difficult decision to break the sacred bond of marriage not on the basis of emotion, but on the basis of reason. This is the substance of what Qur'anic law, the sharia, tells us about divorce, and this is the law which we must obey. For it is God's law, revealed to us through the Prophet Muhammad, may blessings and peace be upon him'" (Fernea 1998:152–153).

As I noted before, in Muslim writings, one finds that the male is depicted as the rational, objective, cool-headed sex. The female is supposedly driven by emotions and is thus unstable. Therefore, it becomes the responsibility of men to handle such weighty matters as the initiation of divorce.

Mohammad Zafeeruddin Nadvi, like Dr. Muhammad, revels in the exaltation of male supremacy. He also outlines practical issues that caution the Muslim man not to be overly hasty in divorcing his wife. "A characteristic of the Islamic divorce law is that the matter of divorce has been entrusted to man. And it is an admitted fact that man is comparatively more far-sighted, more capable of understanding men and matters, has greater tolerance and forbearance and uses his cool common sense in taking decisions" (Nadvi 1982:186).

Muhammad Sharif Chaudhry puts it like this: "No doubt any adult Muslim of sound mind can divorce his wife whenever he desires without assigning any reasons" (Chaudhry 1991:58). Perhaps this is an extreme view, but it happens often. Lamya al Faruqi responds, "Very strict laws have been established in Islamic law to prevent misuse. Unfortunately, these laws have not always been enforced" (Faruqi 1988:72). He goes on to give what he considers to be the Islamic ideal.

"*Talaq* is to be pronounced with specific terms before two qualified witnesses. Each pronouncement must be made at a time when the wife is not incapacitated for sexual activity by menstrual flow. Having made the first statement of divorce, the man must wait to make the second statement until the woman completes her next monthly period. The third pronouncement must be similarly spaced. Only after the third repudiation is the divorce considered final. Each of the other two statements is revocable. The wife continues to live in her home, and she is provided full maintenance throughout the divorce proceedings. During this time, attempts are made to achieve reconciliation through the counseling and arbitration of family and friends. Only if this is not possible is the final pronouncement made and the marriage considered irrevocably broken" (Faruqi 1988:72–73).

At one point in Muhammad's life, there arose great dissension among his wives. These favored women were making extravagant demands. The Prophet became frustrated and threatened to divorce at least some of his wives. It was then that Allah intervened and gave Muhammad guidance. This "revelation" has become part of the Quran.

> O Prophet! Say unto thy wives: If ye desire the world's life and its adornment, come! I will content you and will release you with a fair release. But if ye desire Allah and His messenger and the abode of the Hereafter, then

lo! Allah hath prepared for the good among you an immense reward. O ye wives of the Prophet! Whosoever of you committeth manifest lewdness, the punishment for her will be doubled, and that is easy for Allah. And whosoever of you is submissive unto Allah and His messenger and doeth right, We shall give her reward twice over, and We have prepared for her a rich provision. (Quran 33:28–31)

It is interesting to note how the eternal revelation of Allah, once again, stoops to solve a very temporal problem for the Prophet. Muslim scholars see in this discourse (1) how involved Allah is with his beloved messenger; (2) that Muhammad is allowed to divorce wives who are worldly; (3) that there is punishment or reward for wives, and the choice is theirs to make; and (4) that Muslim wives are to learn from this passage to submit to their husbands and to shun all forms of lewdness.

One Quranic passage has puzzled commentators down through the ages. It says, "And if he hath divorced her (the third time), then she is not lawful unto him thereafter until she hath wedded another husband. Then if he (the other husband) divorce her it is no sin for both of them that they come together again" (Quran 2:230).

Why the in-between husband if the original spouse realizes he made a terrible mistake by uttering the divorce formula? Perhaps he spoke in a fit of anger or even in a state of drunkenness. Now he must wait until his former wife marries and divorces another man. Only then can the original couple remarry. A Tradition reinforces the Quranic verses.

> A man divorced his wife and she married another man who proved to be impotent and divorced her. Then she came to the Prophet and said, "O Allah's Apostle! My first husband divorced me and then I married another man who entered upon me to consummate his marriage but he proved to be impotent and did not approach me except once during which he benefited nothing from me. Can I remarry my first husband in this case?" Allah's Apostle said, "It is unlawful to marry your first husband till the other husband consummates his marriage with you." (7:139; 63.7.190)

This woman is placed in a most difficult position. Most likely she had to divorce the impotent husband and marry another man who is able to consummate the marriage. She then has a choice: To stay with husband number three or divorce him and remarry number one. Quite complicated indeed, and, one wonders, to what purpose?

Female Initiated Divorce

Can one even imagine an abused rural Afghan wife asking her husband for divorce? Most unlikely. Divorce initiatives are usually the prerogative of Muslim men. Islamic scriptures, as found in both the Quran and Hadith, are based on this assumption. It is true that in certain Muslim countries family laws do exist that grant divorce rights to wives, but often they are costly and complicated. Plus there is a huge factor of shame falling on both families if ever a woman does file for divorce.

The norm is that the husband realizes that his marriage is a failure and, therefore, deals with the divorce issue before his wife makes a move. There is a question of honor here for the husband. The man makes initiatives, not the woman whose lot in life is to submit.

There are some grounds, however, for the wife to proceed with divorce. Brooks reports on this in *Nine Parts of Desire.* "For her part, a Muslim woman has no natural right to divorce, and in some Islamic countries no legal way to secure one. The Hanbali school, followed by the Saudis, gives a woman almost no way out of an unhappy marriage without her husband's consent. Shiites and the Sunnis of the Hanafi school allow her to stipulate the right to divorce in her *aqd*, or marriage contract. Shiites, Hanafi and Maliki law all allow a woman's petition on the grounds of her husband's impotence, and Shiites and Malikis also allow petitions on the grounds of failure to provide support, incurable contagious disease or life-threatening abuse. Mental cruelty, nondisfiguring physical abuse or just plain unhappiness are rarely considered grounds on which a woman can seek divorce" (Brooks 1995:60).

In Egypt a wife may apply for a divorce based on grounds of cruelty, but she has to prove that she has been treated in a way that is "intolerable to a person of her social class." One example was given that a slight blow to the body might be within the realm of acceptance for a woman of a poorer class but not for a wife of aristocratic upbringing (Coulson and Hinchcliffe 1978:42).

In some Muslim countries a wife can initiate a divorce if her husband has failed to have sexual relations with her at least once in four months. "The reason: a sexually frustrated wife is more easily tempted to commit adultery, which leads to *fitna* or the social chaos of civil war" (Coulson and Hinchcliffe 1995:39).

Testimonies of Divorce

Malaysia's Former Deputy Prime Minister, Anwar Ibrahim, spoke to the "Women's Day" gathering about the sad plight of many Muslim wives in Malaysia. *Al-Nahdah* magazine reports his comments.

"Deputy Prime Minister Datuk Seri Anwar Ibrahim expressed regret that *Syariah* Courts continued to treat women unfairly and often made decisions in favour of the men mainly because of the chauvinistic attitudes of the officers. 'In the process, women are tortured, abused, tormented and abandoned without alimony,' he said adding that the prejudice against women by these courts would impede Malaysia's aspiration to be a role model for other countries in the implementation of the Islamic laws. 'At the moment, there are thousands of women who have been abandoned or divorced without their knowledge by their husbands, and when these women lodged reports, they had to wait for years before justice was delivered'" (*Al-Nahdah* 1996:69).

This is a sad, but realistic, overview of the condition of many women in Malaysia, which is actually one of the more progressive countries in the Muslim world. Ibrahim, due in part to his outspoken views, has been incarcerated for the past few years in Malaysia.

Jacqueline Pascarl-Gillespie has documented a sad story in her memoir, *Once I was a Princess*. She was wooed by a Malaysian prince and finally convinced to convert to Islam and marry him. Her dreams of riches and happiness soon turned into a grotesque nightmare. On the marriage night, her loving husband became a sexual brute repeatedly raping her while exclaiming, "I can do anything I want with you—you belong to me."

Gillespie expounds on her husband's view of women. She says, "He taught me that under Islamic belief, women were not only the weaker sex, they were also the gender more likely to seduce the other through sheer weakness of morals and inferior intelligence. He explained that women were inherently evil and had to be educated away from their natural inclinations to sin and corruption" (Garceau 2000:L4).

This Asian-Australian woman lived under horrific conditions in Malaysia for five years. She then escaped to Australia with her two children. Her son and daughter were later kidnapped and taken back to Malaysia. Gillespie has not been allowed to see or speak to them for eight years.

On December 8, 2000, Asma Jahngir, a Pakistani woman and human rights lawyer, was interviewed on the BBC program "Hard Talk." Asma told of a woman who came to her office and related a tale of terrible abuse that she had suffered from her husband. As a last resort, the woman was ready to petition for a divorce. During the discussion, a man pushed his way into Asma's office and shot the woman to death. The murderer was a relative; the act an "honor killing."

If not death, then what is the future of the many divorced women? Dr. Saadawi explains what she has seen.

"The day comes when a divorced woman no longer receives her allowance. Often she is left without shelter, constrained to move from one relative's house to another, begging for her meals or seeking a few feet on which to spread her tired body. In many cases she ends up as a domestic servant, a prey to blows, insults and harrowing work that starts at the break of day and extends late into the night, a victim of sexual aggression which she will accept to keep her job and a roof over her head" (Saadawi 1980:200).

Munira, a Saudi Arabian woman of twenty-five years, writes poignantly of that which causes a woman to take the risk of divorce.

> I have lived *and known what it is to smile*
> I have lived *the life of a young girl with hopeful promise*
> I have lived *the life of a young girl who felt the warmth of womanhood*
> I have lived *the feeling of longing for the love of a good man*
> I have lived *the life of a woman whose promise was cut short*
> I have lived *the life of one whose dreams were dashed*
> I have lived *knowing tremendous fear for every man*
> I have lived *through the fears raised by the spectre of an evil coupling*
> I have lived *to see the devil in the guise of a man, ruling my every action*
> I have lived *as a beggar to this man, pleading with him to leave me alone*
> I have lived *to witness my husband have the pleasure of being a man*
> I have lived *to be ravished by the man to whom I was given*
> I have lived *only to endure nightly rapes*
> I have lived *to be buried while still alive*
> I have lived *to wonder why those who claim to love me, helped to bury me*

I have lived *through all of these things, and I am not yet twenty-five years old* (Sasson 1999:279–280).

Who am I, as a Westerner, to judge? Our Western divorce rate hovers at forty-five percent, more or less. The *Los Angeles Times* speculates that there are more than ten million battered wives in America (Parshall 1985:127). And yet abused women in the West have options that are almost non-existent in Muslim society.

Divorce is a terrible reality that leads to untold suffering, deprivation, and dishonor. It is my deepest aspiration and prayer that in both the West and in Muslim countries there might be a new, sustained effort to end the exploitation of fifty-five percent of the world's population to whom every male, Muslim and non-Muslim, owes his existence.

———— 13 ————

Western Converts to Islam

In pursuit of fairness, I have included this chapter on Western women who have become Muslims. Some are from "Christian" backgrounds, and others had little to do with organized religion before converting to Islam. Most have commenced their pilgrimage toward their new faith because of the influence of a Muslim boyfriend or husband.

In light of what I have written leading up to this chapter, it may come as a jolt to realize that there are Western women brought up in a Christian-influenced culture who would consider going under the veil. What about the personal freedoms that must be sacrificed? Parents and friends will surely protest. Even employment may be at risk. However, the fact that Western women do convert is a reality that must be explored.

Conversion

It is appropriate to allow these women to speak for themselves. I have leaned heavily on two books that document testimonies of women who have converted to Islam. One is by B. Aisha Lemu and Fatima Heeren, entitled *Women in Islam*. The other is *Daughters of Another Path* by Carol L. Anway. Names are not given, but the publishers are credible.

The Quran is frequently considered an indecipherable book by the average Western reader. But for one non-practicing Catholic, the Quran was the instrument that led to her conversion.

"My conversion began as the result of a challenge by a Muslim to read the Qur'an in order for us to have a debate on the position of women in Islam. I held the stereotypical view of Muslim women as being oppressed and in a bad position relative to their Christian counter-parts. I was nominally Christian, raised in a Catholic environment, but was not practicing the religion and really only bothered to label myself a Christian in order not to appear too rebellious in front of my extended family (my family was also really only Christian in name, not 'reality').

"The reading of the Qur'an and of hadith of the Prophet is what captured me. I went through a very odd experience whereby for the whole week it took me to read the Qur'an I couldn't sleep and seemed to toss and turn all night in a feverish sweat. I had strange and vivid dreams about religious topics, and when I would get up all I wanted to do was to continue reading the Qur'an. I didn't even study for my final exams which were happening at the same time!" (Anway 1996:34)

This woman felt strongly that, along with the Quran, "strange and vivid dreams" were sent from Allah to bring her to the path of truth. As will be seen in the next chapter, we as evangelicals have felt that we have a corner on how God uses dreams in bringing people to ultimate truth, that is, biblical truth. Now, we see dreams moving women in an opposite direction. And so the enigmas of life continue. Another testimony is from an American woman who married a nominal Muslim. Her quest for understanding God led her away from her Christian upbringing. Both she and her husband then became devout Muslims.

"I started asking a lot of questions from ministers, theologians, and seniors in the field to help me prove Christianity to my husband. I wanted it so badly, I cried to several of them to help me and most of them said, "I'm sorry—I don't know" or "I'll write you," but I never heard from them. The harder I tried to prove Christianity to convert him, the more I moved toward Islam because of its logic, until I finally yielded to the belief and oneness of Allah.

"One thing led to another until my husband and I became practicing Muslims. Islam for me gives me peace of mind because I don't have to understand the Trinity and how God is 'three in one' or that God died on the cross. For me Islam supplies the answers" (Anway 1996:37).

Here is what appears to be a sincere woman whose initial questions were probably raised by her Muslim husband. Sadly, her persistent queries went unanswered. It is not uncommon for the Trinity and the Cross to be major stumbling blocks for Muslims. "Islam supplies the answers," stands as a major indictment to the ministers and theologians who shrugged off this woman's inquiry.

A young intellectual who studied at Purdue University also shares her faith pilgrimage.

"My conversion started when I took a religion class at Purdue University. This first introduction to Islam struck my mind and made more sense (and later, total sense) than other religions I studied. Then I decided to join a study summer tour to Egypt to visit a Muslim country firsthand, to see the mosques, to talk with the people. This opened my mind tremendously. From that point on, Islam was the only way for me to go. When I got back from Egypt, I went to the local mosque, and the sisters helped me begin my path of knowledge and life. In November 1993 I converted and have found peace in my life. Before converting I was not religious. I was drinking and "wild." Islam taught me that this life is the judgment for the after-life and pleasing Allah (SWT) is most important" (Anway 1996:25).

Julie and I have been to Egypt twice and toured rather extensively. We have visited many mosques in that ancient land. Our conversations with the people have been enriching. But we never heard or saw anything that would cause us to desire Islam as our religion of choice. And yet, this highly educated young woman was so gripped by the Islam she experienced there, that she converted, not only cognitively but also behaviorally, giving up the wild life because she "found peace."

In 1999, I saw a CNN special report from Mecca during the Hajj. An attractive, young British woman in full veil was being interviewed. She expressed her satisfaction with being a Muslim. When asked about the Taliban's violations of women's rights in Afghanistan, she replied, "That is not real Islam but rather a cultural aberration." She further stated that she was glad to live in the West and have the freedom to practice true faith.

Debbie Harris, an American from Charlotte, N.C., married a Kuwaiti engineering instructor. She testifies, "Islam has given me such peace of mind. When I accepted Islam it was as if somebody opened my heart and put back in new life." Goodwin documents the process of Debbie's conversion.

"Blond, blue-eyed, and as bubbly as a cheerleader, Debbie met her husband when he was in the United States as a student.

'We dated for six years because Jamal was on a scholarship and the Kuwaiti government does not permit students to marry foreigners; otherwise they lose the scholarship.' Debbie was then a Presbyterian. 'When we married in 1985, I told Jamal I didn't want to convert to Islam, and he said that was okay. But he insisted our children be raised Muslim. When I was pregnant with our first child, I kept asking myself how I could allow a youngster to be raised in a faith I didn't believe in. And so I started to take Islamic classes. As I began to read, I found Islam made a lot of sense. It was not contradictory like my own religion. I didn't convert until 1988, however, because I wanted to wait until all my questions were answered. I had been so confused with Christianity. Whenever I asked questions at my church, I got the runaround. My husband would ask me, 'Why do you believe Jesus is the son of God? Why did God need to send his son? Why did he need a mediator?' And I could only say that is what we believe" (Goodwin 1994:188–189).

In actual fact, Muslims believe Muhammad is a mediator within Islam. He prays for the faithful and for the unfaithful. The problem for Muslims centers more on the title "Son of God." It is repugnant to Muslims to think of Prophet Jesus as a biological son of Allah. His divinity is vehemently denied. The Christian responds by asking the Muslim to ponder the Trinity in more metaphysical terms. Also the concept of mystery is stressed. But, to the average Muslim, these abstractions are irrational and incompatible with the Islamic concept of the pure and uncompromised unity of the one God, who is without partners and has no equal.

One anonymous American wrote of being impressed with the Muslims she met while on a trip to Malaysia. She had always felt out of place in church, so decided to investigate

Islam. Soon she came to the point of conversion, which she describes: "One day I woke with the words, 'OK, I believe, I will go and convert to Islam,' and from that moment on, all of my turmoil and anxiety was gone. All praise to Allah. All of the pain I had felt from past experiences was gone. The nightmares stopped, and I felt the most incredible peace."

Yes "peace," but the question that perplexes the onlooking Christian is, from what source? Was the peace just a relief that she had finally made her decision?

Life after Conversion

The Western woman who converts to Islam often feels she is forced into a defensive position regarding her faith. On one hand, she desires to be a witness for her belief. Conversely, she does not want to be regarded as a societal oddity. In most instances, she will commence wearing the headscarf. In a Western country, that act alone will cause people to look at her with curiosity.

A British convert makes her apologetic for the relevance of Islam: "The present time of widespread rethinking of the role and rights of women is perhaps the appropriate time to look with fresh eyes at the Islamic point of view, which has contributed to the formation of stable societies in both sophisticated and underdeveloped peoples in vast areas of the world over the past fourteen centuries, which has retained the continuity of its principles, and from which the Western world may have something to learn" (Lemu and Heeren 1978:30).

The key words here are that Islam "has contributed to the formation of stable societies." Repeatedly, the defenders of the Muslim faith will compare the divorce rates of Christian and Muslim countries. It is interesting to me how the two camps define morality according to their strengths. In the West it is female freedom; in the Muslim society it is family solidarity. Both groups de-emphasize their failures. In the West, they are infidelity, pornography, and unequal opportunities in the work force. In Muslim society, they are subjugation, the veil, and harsh penalties for any infraction of Islamic law.

The pressure a Western convert feels was expressed by veil-clad American women who were participating in a discussion inside a mosque in Columbia, S.C. I had brought my seminary class to observe their afternoon prayer time. Following the salat, we listened as the female converts talked about how Islam gave them respect and dignity within their new community. Their plea was to be allowed to follow Islam without being made to feel inferior by on-looking Christians. One could sense that they had developed a siege mentality— us against them. Their dress style made their distinctive beliefs obvious, which then led to emotional harassment.

Another difference in many women's lives after converting to Islam concerns marriage. A German convert comments on the stability of arranged marriages.

"What I appreciated by watching how well it is usually working out, is first the custom in Muslim families of so-called arranged marriages. During my stay in a Muslim country,... I could always observe that family life in arranged marriages is far more lasting and stable than in the average Western family. It seems that where parents or relatives with much insight and experience propose marriages, they do it on a broad basis considering family background, education, ambitions, likes and dislikes, and so many other things. And though nearly all Muslim marriages are conducted by buying the cat in the bag (as we say in Germany) which means it is not discovered beforehand whether the partners fit together sexually, as is customary in the West. They can be called far more successful than marriages here" (Lemu and Heeren 1978:41).

Another Western convert explains how she has been able to enjoy a stable marriage by obeying her husband: "The wife herself is responsible for the care of her home and the welfare of her family. She may express her views and make her suggestions concerning all matters, but the best role she can play in keeping the marital tie intact and strong is to recognize her husband as the person responsible for the running of the affairs of the family, and thus to obey him even if his judgement is not acceptable to her...provided he does not go beyond the limits of Islam. This is the meaning of obedience in the context of marriage in Islam. It is a recognition of the role of the husband as the head of the family unit and the loyalty of both husband and wife to a higher law, the Sharia" (Lemu and Heeren 1978:18).

If you deleted the words "Islam" and "Sharia" and replaced them with "Christianity" and "Bible," would you not have a traditional Evangelical understanding of the husband-wife relationship? I use the word "traditional" by design, as there has been a significant shift away from the biblical teaching that a wife is to be submissive to her husband. This is, of course, with the understanding that submission within marriage is to be guided by the higher law of the Bible. So, has Islam spoken attractively to a segment of Western women about these values, which we seldom hear taught in contemporary, Evangelical church services?

Another woman ponders the subject: "Does it not lie in the very nature of a woman that she wants a powerful, just, wise and considerate husband who is capable of taking these decisions? This, I think, is the ideal family life as envisaged by Islam. In such an atmosphere, both partners will find fulfillment in erotic matters as well as in all other matrimonial fields of which rearing children has pre-eminence" (Lemu and Heeren 1978:43).

The adjectives are interesting: powerful, just, wise, and considerate. These are the qualities that this woman finds attractive. Perhaps she found just such a husband who then was able to lead her to Islamic faith.

One convert's testimony highlights her desire for a family life that is truly caring. "Islam grants us within the fold of family life a secure refuge against inward and outward troubles. In a time when people mistrust each other, when everybody thinks of himself first and it is considered a crime to be bothered with the worries of others, only those are well off who know that there is for them at least one place of refuge. Here we may get either good advice or a piece of bread, a helping hand or a bed. Here we can be sure to be defended against the outside world, and we know that the other family members are expecting of us the best and not the worst, which helps us so much to unfold our best qualities. Thus, the family is a marvelous institution for the needy as well as for those who are able to help. No other social institution has so far shouldered similar responsibilities as successfully as the family" (Lemu and Heeren 1978:44).

Muslim families are held in contrast to the impersonal, fast-moving, disconnected families of the West. Interestingly and somewhat surprisingly, one Western woman makes a case for polygamy. She speaks of a situation in which a woman no longer loves her husband but continues to respect him. Her concern is for her own financial security as well as for the welfare of her children. It may be, she further postulated, that the new woman will not want to break up the first family. In this instance, all concerned may regard polygamy a better solution to the problem than either divorce or an extra-marital affair (Lemu and Heeren 1978:29). However farfetched this scenario may seem, it did appeal to this woman. One cannot help but wonder if, faced with the reality of what she described, she herself would agree to such a triangular relationship of intimacy?

Proselytizing

Sharing the Islamic faith with other Westerners is important to most converts. Goodwin talks about twenty-five American women who had married Kuwaitis, become Muslims, and were about to return to the States. A woman by the name of Hind was exhorting these new converts to be a positive witness for Islam.

"Hind opened her class that night with an evangelical theme. 'We are messengers of Islam all around the world,' she told her students as they sat on the floor with her, or on chairs arrayed around the edges of the room. 'You have a great mission before you. When you go to the United States, people will ask why you became Muslims. They will know Islam through you. We are facing rising suspicions globally against Islam. Muslims are being tortured just because they are Muslims. Look at Yugoslavia. When you visit America, don't be afraid when people 'stand in your face' and cause problems for you and your family. Stand firm, let them know what you believe, and they will be affected by you" (Goodwin 1994:183).

I have found Western converts to Islam to be committed, witnessing Muslims. Even if these women are abused and end up divorcing their Muslim husbands, often they continue in the Islamic faith. It would seem that they are willing to cast blame on their spouse, but not on the Muslim faith.

Ida Glaser was speaking to a group of teenage Muslim girls and boys in England about the merits of Christianity when their emotional chanting interrupted her.

"But in the middle of frantic chanting of *'Allahu Akbar'*, 'Allah is Great', I found some comfort when I noticed that there were a few white faces which I thought were Christians. But soon a white girl wrapped in her Iranian-style *chador* reminded me that in today's Britain it is wrong to judge people's religion by the colour of their skin. She had converted to Islam.

"The questions were mainly asked by the Muslim girls and boys. Most of their questions were about the authority of the Bible. But Suzanna, the white girl, changed the course of the discussion by asking, 'I know what Islam has given me as a woman, but what has Christianity to offer?' Before I could answer her question I was bombarded by Muslim girls and boys with all sorts of quotations from their literature to tell the people present how wonderful the religion of Islam was and how good it was towards the women. Again and again they would attack the Bible and say that there was nothing for women in Christian faith or the Bible" (Glaser 1998:xiv–iv).

This young girl was quite willing to testify that she had received from Islam that which Christianity did not offer. There are only two large, organized religions in the world today that promote active witness for their respective beliefs. Thus, Christianity and Islam square off against each other in antagonistic posture. Each is totally convinced of its unilateral claim to unique Truth.

An American who converted to Islam shared these interesting reflections in a letter to a Christian friend.

Washing with water in many religious traditions, including Islam, is a symbol of forgiveness. To make the experience more meaningful, I focus my attention on one of the names of God, one of the divine attributes, at different stages of the process.

As I begin, I repeat the classical invocation, "In the name of God, the Merciful, the Compassionate." Often I feel these words at the level of my heart.

As I wash my hands, I think of God as Friend and Protector (Wali). Then as I rinse my mouth, I ask that I may speak the truth and remember God as Truth (Haq). As I snuffle water in my nose (yes, I've found this washing is a good preventive measure against colds), I recall with the breath, God as the Ever Living One (Hay).

Then I wash my face, including my eyes and think of God as the All Seeing, Insightful One (Basir). As I rinse my left and right arms to the elbow, I recall the strength of God, of the All Powerful One (Al Qadir). Wiping my moistened fingertips across my head, I remember God as All Knowing One (Alim or Khabir). Rinsing my ears, I think of God as the One who Hears All (Sami'a).

No, I do not always recall the names of God in this manner. Still, usually five times a day, I initiate a simple process of baptism and restoration. Each time I seek forgiveness for the many acts we commit constantly in our daily living, of harming ourselves and others, heedlessly or consciously.

Closing I declare there is no God, but God and Mohammed is God's prophet. (Anonymous)

To this woman, Islam has revealed a pertinent and powerful way to worship and remember Allah.

For many converts, the agony of misunderstanding between themselves and their Christian parents is heart wrenching.

"Like my parents, I felt something was being torn from me. One thought kept me from losing hope. Knowing that my parents were believers in the same God I had come to trust and love so much, I would wait for them, and let God help them heal.

"Since I told my family of my conversion to Islam, our relationship has gone through many changes. No doubt it will go through many more. I can honestly say I have never loved and appreciated my parents more than I do now. I would not trade our new relationship for any other" (Saints Herald 1985:18–19,24.)

This breach between faiths will now be much more pronounced since the events of September 11, 2001. Christian parents, even nominal ones, will be aghast at any thought of a relationship developing between their daughter and a

Muslim young man.

One mother describes her reaction upon hearing that her daughter, through the influence of a Muslim boyfriend, had converted to Islam. "Finally we had no more to say to each other. I went to my room, and I sobbed most of the night. Never have I experienced grief like that period of time. I hurt so much that it felt as if something was physically being pulled out of me" (Anway 1996:45).

Feelings of alienation are excruciating to write about. These female converts to Islam counted the cost and made a most difficult decision. It must be said that not all of these women are living in peace and contentment. There are also those who have experienced the inadequacy of Islam and converted (or reconverted) to a vital, saving faith in Jesus Christ.

In the next chapter, I will explore methods to witness to these women and others in the household of Islam.

14

Witness and Conversion

In a sense, what has been written prior to this chapter has been the easy part. Now comes the challenge of struggling with the higher spiritual issues. What is the best way to share our faith with the women of the veil? How can we build bridges into their lives with integrity? What are the points of contact that will open up an understanding of the Gospel? And finally, what evangelistic strategies can we learn from Muslim women who have stepped over the line and converted to Christ?

Witness

One long-term missionary has written about the struggles she experienced in presenting Christ to women of the Muslim diaspora.

"The two major barriers that we found in Muslim women from several different people groups living in Paris are (1) a belief that God is far away and neither interested nor involved in the daily life of a woman, and (2) a belief that sin is something we do and is punished only if we are caught. One woman used the term "spectator" to describe God. In her view, since God is just a spectator and not involved, he sees an individual's sin only when others draw attention to it. Folk Islam, with its animistic practices, provides another strong barrier to the gospel. Other barriers include these characteristics: Muslim women don't feel valued and loved by God. Women don't have the power to make life decisions for themselves. And the image of the father in most Muslim households does not represent accurately the image of Father God. I frequently see mothers teaching their children to hide things from the father. The mother teaches the child that the father is someone to fear, that secrets can be kept and that if the father learns of the behavior, punishment will be swift and severe. When a woman has that image of a father, it is difficult for her to desire to have a relationship with God as Father" (A.H. 2000:161–162).

This is a significant litany of obstacles. And regrettably, it is quite accurate, not only in regard to women in Paris but also throughout the Muslim world. Allah is simply not close, not real, not vital, nor practical to a woman's life. He is an abstract force to be obeyed, not loved. Intimacy with Allah is not a part of a Muslim woman's thinking.

Also I would agree that a Muslim woman cannot enter easily into a realization that God is her heavenly father. Yes, she may love her earthly father. I have seen this deep, loving relationship between Dr. Ali and his daughter. But more often the bond is formal and distant. It is with the mother that a daughter's strongest ties are forged.

Fran Love, the coordinator for Frontiers' women's ministry, shared these practical observations in an article entitled, "Church Planting That Includes Muslim Women."

"Recently I talked with workers in Yemen, Bangladesh, China, Mauritania, and Turkey. When I asked why women had not come to Christ, I found several reasons: First, the attitude of many Muslim men to Muslim women is that they are creatures who are neither worthy of nor interested in spiritual matters. Typically, a Muslim convert will say when questioned why he doesn't bring his wife to a Christian gathering, 'She is a woman, she wouldn't understand.' Sadly, our missionaries reinforce this stereotype when they complain that Muslim women aren't interested in talking about God. Missionary women especially become frustrated at trying to bring God into their conversations with Muslim women who would, they say, rather talk about the price of vegetables at the market, babies, cooking, and methods of birth control" (Love 1996:135).

My wife has found these observations typical of women in Bangladesh. One has to understand the normal ritual of life for a rural Muslim woman. Housekeeping, bearing children, cooking, and wifely duties occupy not only her time but also her thoughts. Julie struggled, mostly with little success, to get the women beyond their confined worldview of earthly concerns and into meaningful spiritual conversation. They failed to see the relevance. The brush-off that was commonly given is "I was born a Muslim, I will die a Muslim."

When finally we began to see men coming to Christ in Bangladesh, we immediately gave them Bible teaching regarding the way they treat their wives. We urged them to stop wife beating and then, through their changed lives, bear witness to the new birth. This was followed by an exhortation to their wives to personally receive Christ as Savior. But the men were exactly as Fran depicted. They asked, "How can a mere wife ever understand these profound truths? She is so ignorant. All she is capable of grasping are household concerns." It took a number of years before we began to see the men change their attitudes and actually win their wives to the Lord. It is still a slow process, but at least it is happening.

Miriam Adeney has listed a number of topics that can possibly be springboards for opening a conversation about Christ with a Muslim.

> Jesus' story
> Earthy, biblical symbols—bread, water
> Women in Scripture
> Psalms, Proverbs, parables, Bible narrative
> God's names, Jesus' names
> Women of history and today
> Charms
> Veil
> Fasting
> Creed
> Submission
> Dreams
> Sacrifice feasts, especially Abraham
> Fulfilled singleness
> Pornographic videos: what Christians think about sex
> Child-raising
> Family planning
> Solving family conflicts
> Community social ethics
> God's creation, ecology
> Cultures: God-given creativity and sinful exploitation
> Repentance for Western sins
> Christ versus Christians
> Forgiveness

Confidence
Love
Release from anger
Power to do right
(Love 2000:121–122)

Context will determine which of these subjects will have relevance in different scenarios. Urban versus rural, literate versus illiterate, single versus married, mystical versus orthodox, and rich versus poor. These are all areas where sensitivity will need to be exercised.

Another unique witness involves singing the Scriptures. Missionary Julia Colgate found a creative way to do this. "My husband and I have enjoyed many opportunities to sing the Scriptures to our Muslim hearers. If we are invited to offer a song at a wedding reception or a house-warming ceremony, we often choose a rendition of 1 Corinthians 13, Psalm 23, or Psalm 103 arranged in a musical style that the people here appreciate. We trust that the living Word of God will do its work in the hearts of our hearers. Music carries the truth of God and the joy of the Gospel so beautifully. When Scripture is joined to melodies and chord progressions that make sense to the Eastern ear, hearts seem to soften much faster than when we simply open the Bible and read aloud" (Colgate n.d.:15).

One of the important observations here is the importance of using melodies that Muslim women will appreciate. All too frequently Western hymns are adapted to the local languages, but the tunes are not changed. The result is that there is no real communication or impact. Chanting also can be used in certain situations.

Hospitality is an important element of Muslim culture.

One missionary relates how she used her home to facilitate meaningful relationships. "Over the years, we have invited friends and neighbors to many open-house/thanksgiving ceremonies in our home. In this context, we have had the opportunity to honor publicly, in culturally appropriate ways, the ones who have become dear to us. On these occasions, we have tried our best to make our home comfortable to our guests by moving furniture, and by setting out ashtrays for the many smokers here. We have always offered a room with a prayer rug and ladies' prayer coverings at the time of the call to prayer, if anyone indicated that he or she wanted to pray. Rather than having to go home to do what they customarily did, they could stay. They knew their prayers would not interrupt our time together. They would finish, fold up the rug, and we would simply continue. By exercising some understanding and tolerance of their customs and habits, we were able to further our relationships" (Colgate n.d.:8).

Another ministry tactic is not only to provide a place for prayer but also to pray with a Muslim friend. As one missionary stated, "Don't say, 'I'll pray for you later,' if you have opportunity to pray now! Pray for every need. Pray for the sick. Ask God for healing in Jesus' name. Our offer to pray is an expression of love that is quite rare. This love will minister to her spirit, at the very least" (Colgate n.d.:16).

Another missionary woman went through the complete prayer ritual with her Muslim house helper.

"It was a fascinating experience to kneel beside Anisa on my mat, positioned a little behind her so I could follow her movements. I observed intensely and also prayed intensely for Anisa that Jesus would reveal Himself to her even during the minutes she carried out her Muslim duty in my home. After her prayers in Arabic, Anisa prayed in her own language, and I understood her words of thanks for the love of my family toward her. It was very touching for me to hear her pray with tears. When she was finished, we looked at each other and hugged. Then we stood up, unpinned our coverings and folded the prayer rugs. The night and morning were a precious experience that helped to cement our mutual understanding and love" (Colgate n.d.:23–24).

As one who has prayed with Muslim men, I can say this willingness to pray together is much appreciated. Before I started praying with Dr. Ali, he viewed me as a more secular person. But when we commenced corporate prayer his comment was, "Phil, now I know you are a man of God. You are seeking God like me." It opened many opportunities for in-depth discussions about our respective faiths.

I had reservations about performing the salat in the exact manner that Muslims did. Instead, I sat on the floor with uplifted hands while my Muslim friend went through his unique-to-Islam prayer ritual. Also, I did not want to convey the idea that I gave complete assent to all of the content of Islamic prayers. This can be done with tact and sensitivity.

One other style of ministry to Muslim women that we have engaged in is to provide a dorm for students and professionals in Manila. Space is provided for twelve women. Two Christian women, who feel that this is their special calling, oversee the dorm. Cooking facilities, a television, and a computer are provided. The Muslim women pay a reasonable monthly rent. Many good conversations have taken place about religious issues between the boarders and our staff.

Other ministries to women, such as student outreaches, youth centers, computer schools, medical assistance programs, English classes, baking instructions, and micro enterprise projects all have potential for witnessing. The first thing to do is to research felt needs and go from there. It would be my firm conviction that ministry should be woman to woman. Too often serious problems have risen from cross-gender witnessing between Christians and Muslims.

Instruments of Conversion

God does indeed move in mysterious ways. The variety of conversion stories could be likened to a kaleidoscope. Multi-faceted are the experiences of coming into a relationship with Christ. All valid, and, in some measure, all unique. I share here just a sampling of these accounts.

In the Philippines, Mia shared a room with a born-again Christian. She had never been that close to a Christian before. Judy prayed often, even in front of Mia. She did this by kneeling at her bedside. One day Mia overheard Judy weeping softly and praying aloud for her conversion. It was a moment that would haunt her for years.

Discouragement and deep depression invaded Mia's life. She moved to Manila and did odd jobs. She had no peace or direction. She even contemplated suicide. There was nothing to live for. Despair and gloom were taking her in a downward spiral toward self-destruction.

One afternoon Mia was walking down a street near a large Muslim community. There before her on the sidewalk were two Americans sitting behind tables of literature. She queried these men as to the purpose of their activity. George, one of the men, suggested that Mia go inside the small reading room where his wife, Sharon, would be happy to chat with her.

Immediately, Sharon and Mia felt a bond develop between them. Mia was invited to help Sharon learn her Muslim language. Literally hundreds of hours were spent together.

Gradually Sharon's lifestyle and articulated witness began to powerfully impact Mia. She could not easily discard the memory of her Christian roommate, and now the gracious witness of her new American friend. One special day Mia counted the cost and bravely accepted Christ into her life.

Mia is a member of one of the most solidly Muslim ethnic groups in the Philippines. She is from a people group that boasts, "Never will any of our Muslims become a despised Christian. Never!" And so Mia is a trophy of grace. She has won several family members to the Lord and is one of the most vibrant, dynamic female converts in all of the Philippines. This story is especially precious to me as I was the other American sitting behind the tables of literature.

Another young woman has allowed me to share her testimony with you.

"I am Fatima, and I was born and raised in an Asian country. I grew up in a Muslim family, the second child among six girls. Ever since I was little, I believed in Islam. I considered myself loyal to the faith. I went to the mosque every Friday and was faithful in keeping the Ramadan Fast. But in spite of that, I was considered the black sheep of the family. I went through school with flying colors. I was always at the top of the class. I wasn't close to my parents and seldom went out with friends. I was always nagging my sisters and was the type of person who fought when I knew I was right— very confrontational.

"My father used to work in the capital city as a security guard at a bank. I visited him in 1994, and he brought me to my uncle's home. That was the first time I met Ruth and Anna (because they were renting one of my uncle's apartments). I took a three-month computer course with them, and Ruth asked me to teach her my Muslim language in return.

When I had problems, I would go to them and they gave me good advice. Whenever they would leave, they would hand their keys over to me with the instruction that I could read any magazines or books in their apartment. I saw the Bible and started reading it. I found out that Ruth's advice came from the Bible, so I said to myself, 'It must be a good book!' For seven months, I witnessed their lives and continued reading the Bible. They did not actually share God's word about salvation with me, but I was so impressed with their way of life.

"I could not help but ask my two new friends about the Bible. It was my own move. They did not insist on sharing God's Word like everyone else does. By then I knew that something unique was happening to me. That was Ruth and Anna's 'go signal' from the Lord to share the Gospel with me. They did it very carefully, so that I would not be offended. In October 1994, I accepted Jesus (*Isa Almasih*) into my life as my personal Savior and Lord.

"For days after that, I felt so guilty! Why did I make such a decision? I felt I was not loyal to Islam anymore! I sought to become a better Muslim. I went to the mosque more often and prayed the same prayer, 'God, if my decision is correct, then give me peace and joy in my heart. Show me the true path.' The Lord assured me of His peace and gave me joy in my heart. The doubt slowly faded away as we continued studying the Bible together. I am so thankful to the Lord that I met Ruth and Anna. *Alhamdulillah!* (Praise the Lord)!"

I can speak for the veracity of this testimony. There are several important components to Fatima's spiritual pilgrimage that are worth noting. Ruth and Anna were extremely trusting Christians. Few Americans would hand over the keys to their home to a Muslim. This act of trust and love communicated deeply to Fatima. The two women did not immediately press the claims of Christ on Fatima. They made literature available and waited patiently for the Holy Spirit to do His work of grace in her heart.

Post-conversion doubt and struggling is not uncommon. Fatima sought Christian confirmation by going deeper into Islamic ritual. "Where is the true path?" she asked. She earnestly sought Truth and, after a period of time, came into a peace and joy that she had never known. This period was followed by effectively witnessing to her family. Today, I know her as a radiant believer.

A Lebanese girl converted to Christ and later was asked about the influence of literature in her life. She answered, "Well, I think that just taking a pamphlet and reading it won't do a lot because you have to understand much more than just reading that you have to be saved. You have to really see it in others" (Mirza 1970:12–13). This is not to disparage the value of Christian literature, but it almost always needs to be used in tandem with a Christian's life and testimony.

Mina grew up in a wealthy home in East Africa. Her entire family was Muslim. She had twin brothers whom she dearly loved. In a miraculous sequence of events, these young men read one of Hal Lindsay's books on future world judgment, went to their respective rooms to go to bed, and both prayed to receive Christ. They got up the next morning and quickly went to share their new life in Christ with each other. Same biological and spiritual birthdays; two new members of the Kingdom!

Immediately they went to work on Mina. It was shocking for her to hear that her beloved twin brothers had become Christians, but their loving witness was powerful. Mina went to Canada for study and there met a pastor's daughter who helped bring her to faith.

Today Mina is married and she and her husband are serving in northern Russia working among Muslims. A number of her family members have become believers. The twins are active Christian businessmen in south Florida. Trophies of grace.

A touching story comes out of Pakistan where two dedicated American missionary women labored for many years in an unbelievably hot, dusty, and hostile environment. In an unpublished book, one of the missionaries writes about a simple Pakistani woman who insisted that she had to memorize the name of Jesus.

"We gave Bahar free medical treatment at the dispensary, but it was soon clear that for this poor, old widow God had more in mind than medical help.... Though she was old and illiterate, her mind was being activated by the Holy Spirit. Faithfully, she came each day to be treated despite the six-mile walk to and from her home.

"One day she seemed deeply disturbed about something. When we asked her, 'Is something troubling you today, Bahar?' she answered with a perplexed frown, 'Yes, I cannot remember His name.'

"'Whose name?'" we questioned.

"'Why, the name of the Son of God who loved me and died for me. I've believed on Him in my heart, He's given my heart peace and eternal life, but I can't remember His name. I know you've told me many times, but I'm just a poor, illiterate country woman, and I can't remember.'

"That day she sat like a little girl on the edge of the rope bed, swinging her legs back and forth as she memorized that beautiful name. 'The Lord Jesus Christ, the Lord Jesus Christ. I think I can remember it now.' Then with a radiant face, she left to share this Lord Jesus Christ with others" (Ilaim n.d.:17). It was a massive hassle to translate the JESUS film into one Asian Muslim language, but the missionaries persisted. Just one testimony is shared here of how that film has brought women to Christ.

"In Islam there were many beliefs that I didn't understand. There were teachings that puzzled me because they were in contradiction with goodness. This bothered me so I asked the Lord, 'Lord, why do you have teachings that cause trouble for people? Why must people get hurt so that your commands are followed? We are all your children which you have created.' After that I wanted to cry. I began to ask about God's word until someone shared with me about the true teachings of the Lord. I was satisfied with what she said so I was forced to think about it. Then I saw the Jesus film. I almost cried when I found out that the teachings of Jesus answered all my former questions. There was only one thing to do: to receive and obey Christ's teachings. Since that time the confusion and anger have been removed from my heart. I have a quietness inside now and almost every area of my life has changed. I have become close to Jesus and his love overflows from my heart. Now I have given my life to him and I know that wherever I am he will never leave me."

In our Manila Reading Center, we show the JESUS film in a Muslim dialect four afternoons a week. Filipino Muslim women are quite free-spirited and move around in Manila without veil or head covering. They often come into the Center to watch our film. They are deeply impressed with the scenes of the Cross. We can only pray these impressions will lead to actual conversions.

At times the traditional Christian church is an instrument of conversion, as it was with this Arab woman. She had a problem with alcohol and came into a relationship with a spirit.

"The spirit told her not to behave as a Christian, meaning the use of alcohol and cigarettes, and to pray her prayers. For the next eleven years she served this spirit, whom she called 'my father' as he called her 'my daughter.' This spirit was a demanding spirit. To grant his favors he required gifts from Aysha. She says that he would ask her what she had and then demand her to give it to him. But he gave virtually nothing in return. This went on until she had nothing left. Then the spirit and the sheiks drove her away. Aysha began to question if this spirit was truly from God. 'Would God see only my hand instead of looking upon my heart?'

"She then set out to find the truth. She met some Christian women and went to the Living Word Church's worship services and heard the gospel. Aysha says that she received Jesus and was freed from the torment of these spirits" (A.H. 1998:34).

Perhaps the church had what the woman regarded as strange ritual and sermon content. But the Lord spoke to this woman in her desperation to be freed from the influence of evil spirits.

Another thrilling conversion story about a woman with leprosy comes out of Jerusalem. Ralph Freed reports this in his book, *Reach Arabs for Christ.*

"Signs of leprosy appeared, and the people of the village knew that I was a leper. They pronounced me unclean and drove me out of the village. I came to another village outside of the East wall of Jerusalem where there was a group of lepers.... One day the members of the colony decided that they would marry me to one of the men who also was a leper.... When they could not persuade me, they beat me and put me in stocks.

"My brother, who was a Moslem priest, used to visit me. One day he told me about one of the prophets of old, called Isa (Jesus) who in His day used to perform many miracles and healed many lepers.... My brother said, 'I wish that Isa could be here. He would have compassion on you and heal you.' After this I always longed that Isa could live now and help me.

"I was still lying in the stocks...when an American lady came with an interpreter. She asked me why I was treated this way. I told her. She asked me, 'Do you believe that Christ can heal you?' Then she told me the wonderful story of the Saviour who can save and heal. She told me that she wanted to take me to her home if I was willing. They let me go and I went to live with her in Jerusalem. She gave me some black medicine. Then she and another lady prayed for me.... After three months an American doctor came to us.... He took some of my blood and went away. A few months later, after his arrival in America, he wrote that they examined my blood and that I had no trace of leprosy left. I was healed!

"Oh, what a wonderful feeling it was after more than five years of awful suffering. I know that the medicine could not have effected the healing in such a short time. It was the Lord Jesus Christ Himself.... It has been now about forty years since the Lord healed me and saved me. I am still living in my native village testifying to the power of Christ" (Freed 1972:44–46).

How uniquely the Holy Spirit works. The words of a Muslim priest brother and the selfless, loving care of a missionary combine to cause this leprous woman to humbly seek the healer, not only of her body but also of her soul.

Dreams

In the late sixties, while living in Bangladesh, we began to hear of the exciting conversion experience of Bilquis Sheikh. Her husband had been the Minister of Interior in united Pakistan. They had been divorced for five years when Bilquis had her unique encounter with Christ. It all started with a dream.

"Normally I never dream, but this night I did. The dream was so lifelike, the events in it so real, that I found it difficult the next morning to believe they were only fantasy. Here is what I saw.

"I found myself having supper with a man I knew to be Jesus. He had come to visit me in my home and stayed for two days. He sat across the table from me and in peace and joy we ate dinner together. Suddenly, the dream changed. Now I was on a mountaintop with another man. He was clothed in a robe and shod with sandals. How was it that I mysteriously knew his name, too? John the Baptist. What a strange name. I found myself telling this John the Baptist about my recent visit with Jesus. 'The Lord came and was my guest for two days,' I said. 'But now He is gone. Where is He? I must find Him! Perhaps you, John the Baptist, will lead me to Him?'

"That was the dream. When I woke up I was loudly calling the name, 'John the Baptist! John the Baptist!'" (Sheikh 1978:35)

Bilquis lived in a palatial home in northwest Pakistan with her grandson, Mahmud. She had many servants to cater to her every whim. Her personality was strong, even aggressive. She was used to getting her way. Now she is confronted with an enigma. Who is this John the Baptist? Calling her driver, she demanded that they go immediately to the nearby home of Dave and Synnove Mitchell, missionaries with The Evangelical Alliance Mission (TEAM). Synnove, looking out her window and seeing Bilquis, felt a tinge of apprehension. What was this wealthy Pakistani woman doing, coming with strident step, up her walkway? After being invited in, Bilquis, never being one for small talk, quickly got to the point, 'Do you know who John the Baptist is?' Synnove then began to share with Bilquis not only about John, but also about the One to whom he pointed. Bilquis listened with rapt attention. Gratefully receiving the literature Synnove gave her, she returned to her home. What happened a few days later can only be explained as a supernatural visitation from on High.

"Then one evening as I relaxed before the fire, I found myself picking up the Bible again...I had read straight through all the Gospels and the Book of Acts, and that night I had reached the last book in the Bible. I was fascinated by Revelation, even though I understood very little of it. I read as if directed, strangely confident. And then abruptly I came to a sentence that made the room spin. It was the twentieth verse of the third chapter of Revelation:

"See, I stand knocking at the door. If anyone listens to my voice and opens the door, I will go into his house and dine with him, and he with me.

"And dine with Him, and He with me! I gasped, letting the book fall in my lap.

"This was my dream, the dream where Jesus was having dinner with me! At the time I had had no knowledge of a book called Revelation. I closed my eyes and once again I could see Jesus sitting across the table from me. I could feel His warm smile, His acceptance. Why, the glory was there too! Just as it had been with the Father. It was the glory that belonged to His Presence!

"Now I knew that my dream had come from God. The

way was clear. I could accept Him, or reject Him.... I would have to make my full decision *now*, one way or the other.

"I made up my mind and knelt in front of the fire.

"'Oh God, don't wait a moment. Please come into my life. Every bit of me is open to You.'... I had said yes. Christ was in my life now, and I knew it" (Sheikh 1978:55–56).

Not only is this a beautiful story, but it has also lasted. Some time after her conversion, Bilquis, along with her beloved grandson, Mahmud, immigrated to America. She purchased a lovely home in Thousand Oaks, California.

As we had met her in Pakistan, I thought it would be good to see Bilquis in her new setting. Julie and I called for an appointment and made our way to her home during one of our visits to California. Soon we were chatting away with Bilquis. Her great desire was to see Americans revived and experiencing the reality of Christ as she had. Most of her time was spent speaking in churches and also writing her best-selling book, *I Dared to Call Him Father*.

At a very old age, Bilquis journeyed back to Pakistan to die in the land of her birth. Met by many relatives at the Lahore airport, these were her first words: "You all think I have returned here to again embrace Islam before I die. Let me assure you, I am a Christian and I will die as a Christian. Now...let's go and have lunch."

Bilquis has gone to be with her Lord whom she loved supremely. Her spiritual pilgrimage all began with a profound dream that impacted her for all time and eternity.

A Christian doctor had been able to win an Indonesian man to Christ. One day he shared these words with the new believer.

"'Before I baptize you, I would like for you to publicly confess your newfound faith in Christ. May I suggest that you do this with your wife.' The new convert was quite distraught. Any type of public confession meant that he would be ostracized from his family and could mean that he would pay the ultimate price for his faith.

"He went home a little discouraged, not knowing what to do. That night his wife had a dream. In her dream she saw a beautiful garden surrounded by a fence. There was a gate and at the gate stood a gatekeeper. She could see her husband sitting in the garden but she was outside. She started to proceed through the gate into the garden, but the gatekeeper stopped her and said, 'Excuse me, you can't come in here.' She said, 'No, you don't understand. I want to be with my husband.' The gatekeeper said, 'Your husband is a Christian and can be here, but you are not, so you cannot join him in the garden.' She awoke, rolled over, shook her husband, looked him in the eyes and said, 'Why didn't you tell me you had become a Christian? I want to become a Christian too.'

"Very early the next morning, the two of them went to the doctor's house and explained the dream. After a few hours the woman invited Jesus into her heart and she too became a Christian. A few weeks later the husband and wife were baptized together in a river near their home" (R. Love 2000:157–158).

The truth of the dream was a powerful influence in this woman's life. It would be unreasonable to explain away this nocturnal encounter as a mere coincidence.

The dream of an Iranian woman, Esmat, started her on a salvation journey. "One night Esmat had a dream. Earlier that day, a brother had prayed for her, with beautiful words and kind eyes. 'Why can't the mullahs' eyes back home look like that?' she asked herself as she went home. Why couldn't they convey that kind of love? That night she dreamt she was in Iran, going down the street dressed in her chador (head covering). She had to go through a narrow passage lined by rows of armed guards on both sides. They were like walls hemming her in. 'I want to be free!' she cried to the Lord. At once the walls fell down, and the face of the man who had prayed for her that day showed through the broken wall" (Adeney 2000:111).

A Filipino woman in one of our outreaches had this dramatic dream. She had gone to a beautiful place and saw multitudes of people of different nationalities. There, she saw a dead man wrapped in white cloth and His blood kept coming out of His body, flowing towards the people. But nobody noticed Him except her. She succinctly stated, "I saw the Man." Sara explained to her that the blood of Jesus washed away the sins of the world. It is for everyone including Muslims like her. Meah said that even if her mind commanded her not to pray to Isa, her heart's voice was louder saying "Isa, Isa, ISA..." So she followed her heart.

A Korean missionary in Thailand wrote to me about a Muslim student who had a dream about a distinctive looking man whom she did not recognize. A year later she saw a picture of Christ and immediately understood that this was the man of her dreams. She sought out a church and within three months became a Christian.

A Filipino Muslim had become a believer. He was anxious to lead his wife to the Lord. This is their story as told to me.

"The couple talked into the night. Datu couldn't believe his wife's receptivity to the good news. They fell asleep but around midnight Sara shook Datu awake. She was afraid. 'I just had a dream.... I dreamed about the prophet Jesus, the God of the Christians. I was riding a horse along the side of a mountain and I met my cousin's wife also riding a horse on her way to the market. I asked her to buy me some fish and then I continued my journey. I don't know if I was walking or riding. Then I realized I was being followed and as I looked behind me I saw a beautiful woman. I thought that she was the mother of Jesus. She was dressed in a black hooded robe but her face glowed and she was carrying a cross high over her head. Because I was so afraid I started walking faster without a rest. Wherever I went, the lady followed.

"I started to run and found myself entering a temple for only women. Someone questioned me, 'How did you get into the temple. Only those who believe in the One nailed on the cross are able to enter.' Then she asked me if I was a Christian and I answered, 'Yes, I am.' When she heard my answer, she gave me something to eat, and as I ate it I knew that I would live forever. I also noticed that the woman following me was nowhere to be seen.

"I went home and gave some of this special food to my mother. 'I ate this,' I told her, 'as a sign that I am a follower of the One that was nailed on the cross and I will not die!' My mother listened intently and then suggested we both go back to the temple together. When my mother took me by my hand to leave, I woke up."

Both husband and wife are now solid believers and have been baptized together.

So what do we do to facilitate dream conversions? There appears to be but one response to this conundrum, and that is to pray fervently for the Lord to visit Muslim women in their moments of slumber. Then we must stand ready to give scriptural interpretations to those who inquire as to meanings.

One could wish for many more conversion stories of Muslim women, but the exciting thing is that it is happening, and probably in record numbers. For that we give thanks to God!

15

Discipleship

Sometimes when I share with women the message of Christ, I shudder to think of the consequences for them if they choose to follow him. I know the suffering it may cause them. For all of us in this situation, it is imperative that we are absolutely certain of the truth of our words. There must be no doubt in our minds because we are calling these women to a costly commitment. (Smith 2000:135)

I personally ponder these thoughts deeply. The assurance of eternal life may also include a death certificate. Entrance into a heavenly kingdom may mean leaving this earthly kingdom. Receiving internal peace and joy may involve enduring emotional perplexity and confusing mystery. Physical abuse often follows a simple verbal declaration of faith. And if this statement is true for men, it is much more accurate for women.

"For we are to God the aroma of Christ among those who are being saved and those who are perishing. To the one we are the smell of death; to the other, the fragrance of life. And who is equal to such a task?" (II Corinthians 2:15–16). These are penetrating words.

Few Muslim women have the freedom to safely and comfortably exchange their Islamic faith for a relationship with Jesus Christ. Those who are agents of change among other Muslim women feel the crushing weight of this responsibility and privilege. Our faith is at stake. The Word of God has spoken. The line of demarcation between life and death is clear. Though we shudder to think of the possible consequences of our shared message, we are closed off against alternative options.

We feel our inadequacy as expressed in the words "and who is equal to such a task?" But in the strength of Christ, we are compelled to go forth. After salvation comes the imperative of sustained discipleship.

First Steps in Discipleship

Upon receiving salvation in Christ, Bilquis Sheikh felt she had to deal with the biblical command concerning water baptism. She asked her servant, Raisham, to assist her.

"And thus on January 24, 1967, began a most unusual baptism....

"'Yes, Raisham,' I said again. 'Please fill the tub.'

"She turned to her duty, a puzzled expression on her face; never had I taken a bath at this hour of the day.

"Raisham announced that my tub was ready; I dismissed her. What I proceeded to do may have some theological problems. But I wasn't thinking in theological terms. I was simply trying to be obedient to a strong urge, which was backed up by Scripture. I was supposed to be baptized *now*, and with the impediments that I felt marshalling themselves,

I had doubts about waiting even until the afternoon.

"So, because I wanted more than anything else in the world to stay in the Lord's Presence, and the way to do that was through obedience, I walked into the bathroom and stepped into the deep tub. As I sat down, water rose almost to my shoulders. I placed my hand on my own head and said loudly: 'Bilquis, I baptize you in the name of the Father and of the Son and of the Holy Ghost.' I pressed my head down into the water so that my whole body was totally immersed.

"I arose from the water rejoicing, calling out, and praising God. 'Oh Father, thank you. I'm so fortunate.' I *knew* that my sins had been washed away and that I was acceptable in the sight of the Lord" (Sheikh 1978:76–77).

Bilquis read the Word of God and felt she had to act upon it. She understood the significance of her action. Other women have come to this watershed moment of their spiritual lives and turned back. And who can blame them? To many on-looking Muslims, baptism is a declaration of denial—a denial of one's parents, extended family, friends, and acquaintances. It is the ultimate act of a traitor. One's country and religion have been terribly maligned. Shame. Dishonor. Disrespect. In some Muslim contexts, the only way to restore familial dignity is to arrange an honor killing of the female convert.

How, then, does one give counsel in regard to baptism? Some support a secret rite while others suggest that it be performed in a distant city. A few postulate an alternative: a waterless ceremony of "initiation." In most instances, baptism is delayed until church elders or missionaries agree upon proof of conversion.

For Bilquis, her next private encounter with God was to be the filling of the Holy Spirit. The first people she shared her experience with were David and Synnove Mitchell.

"When David met us at the door of the Mitchells' house, the scent of delicious cooked foods floated around him, and laughter sounded from within the room.

"'Come in! Come in!' he exclaimed, drawing us into the living room filled with a holiday spirit. A Christmas tree glowed in the corner and the laughter of the two Mitchell children, just a little older than Mahmud, rang out from another room. Mahmud happily joined them at their play.

"I could not contain my joy any longer. 'David!' I cried, using his first name without thinking. 'I am a Christian now! I have been baptized in the Holy Spirit!'

"He stared at me for a moment, then drew me into the house. 'Who told you about the Holy Spirit Baptism?' he asked, his gray eyes wide. He began laughing joyously and praising God. Hearing his 'Hallelujah!' Synnove rushed into the room from the kitchen and David again asked: 'Who told you?'

"'Jesus told me,' I laughed. 'I read it in the Bible's Book of Acts; I asked God for it and received it.'

"Both David and Synnove looked bewildered. But then suddenly they rushed to me. Synnove put her arms around me and broke into tears. David joined her. Then the three of us stood there, arms around each other, praising God for what He had done" (Sheikh 1978:58–59).

I'm sure David and Synnove were quite astonished as they watched Bilquis interact with the Lord in such an unorthodox fashion. First, self-baptism and then Holy Spirit baptism, all without human guidance. The Mitchells had determined that their discipleship role was to be that of encouragement. In no way were they going to pour cold water on the flames of new-found faith.

There is agreement on the necessity of a vibrant work of the Holy Spirit in the life of the convert. How this is taught, understood, and applied will vary among Christian groups. Some will stress a post-salvation, one-time sanctification experience, while others will teach that maturing in Christ is a life-long process. To all, holiness is the goal. There should be no avoidance of teaching about the Holy Spirit just because of differences in understanding. The new believer must come to an acceptance and appropriation of the Spirit's empowerment for life and witness.

Cultural Barriers

Illiteracy is a major problem among Muslim women. Author A.H. comments on this.

"Most Muslim women are oral communicators. Some Muslim countries educate girls but do so in schools that teach by rote memory, which doesn't encourage thinking and analysis. Research has shown that people who study in these types of schools and don't continue to read after finishing become functionally illiterate in just a few years. The girls leave school, marry and start their families. Most of them don't continue to read, and after several years of non-reading, they revert to a preferred learning style of oral communication.... During eleven years in Gaza, I met one female nursing student who read for pleasure, and she did that in English because it was easier than Arabic" (A. H. 2000:147).

All of the above is common throughout the Muslim world. For many girls, education is limited to a year or two in the *Madrassa* (a school that emphasizes Quranic studies). In non-Arabic speaking countries, this educational opportunity is often confined to learning how to read Arabic. This is done with little or no comprehension of content.

Missionaries who disciple illiterate Muslim women have two basic choices. The first is to accept the status quo and emphasize oral communication, repetition, and memorization. This can be done, but it is slow and also depends on the physical presence of the discipler. The other option is to begin a literacy class. This too is slow and requires a skilled teacher. But its returns are greater. After a period of time, the believer is able to grow spiritually through self-study. Dependence shifts from a person to written materials.

Receiving family permission to teach an illiterate convert may be extremely difficult. The father or husband frequently refuses to allow the woman to forsake her household duties. He puts little or no value on a woman's need to learn to read or write. One option around this is to share Bible study cassette tapes with the convert.

Fran Love speaks to another approach for discipleship.

"A missionary couple working in Central Asia took care to honor older women by pairing women leaders. If the gifted leader was a young single woman, she was asked to co-lead with an older married woman who would bring stability and experience to the group and credibility to the younger leader.

"In one MBB church, two educated, single women were sent away to learn about Evangelism Explosion. Because it was not fitting for them to teach what they had learned within a public setting to MBB married men, these two women taught the principles to the married couple in leadership. The male leader passed on what he learned to the men in the church; similarly, the woman leader taught the women in the church. This honored both the spiritual gifts of the single women and the culture's values" (Love 2000:204).

There must be great care to segregate the sexes in most teaching situations. This is particularly true in rural settings. In Bangladesh the women sat on the verandah and listened while the men led and participated in their worship meeting inside the bamboo hut. It was extremely difficult to gather the women together for a "women only" meeting.

In one Asian country, a curtain provided segregation for men and women. "We held meetings separately until after our first baptism. After that, we started out with the men on one side of the meeting room and the women on the other side. After the first month, the men said, 'We must have a curtain down the center of the room. We are getting men off the street who only want to see our beautiful sisters, and that is not right.' So we have worshiped for years with a curtain down the center and men and women in the same room. When we have communion service or a teaching service, we have men and women meeting at separate times, but the worship service is together" (Jansen 2000:196).

There are more liberated situations where women can gather freely with men for Bible studies. These opportunities are most often found in cities and large towns. Even so, caution must be exercised. One of the most natural ways to proceed is within the context of house churches.

"There are numerous advantages for women through the house church structure, several of which are: (1) House churches will usually form around family networks and so are places where women can [be] most comfortable. This is their domain, and where they feel safe with people they know. (2) House churches depend less on one teacher and more on participatory discussion. In this atmosphere, women are encouraged to ask questions and to share insights. (3) House churches focus less on having church services and more on the transformational ministries of changing lives. In this context, a Muslim woman can ask for and receive help in any area of her life, knowing too that her husband and children or other family members will be receiving the same attention and help. But perhaps the single most important advantage is the natural environment a house church gives for women to develop their gifts and leadership, ingredients necessary to the reproduction of church" (Love 1996:138).

This overview is true, but it all depends on the wife having an agreeable husband. There will be little chance for this approach to work without the explicit permission of the spouse. However, most women who are married have come to Christ following the conversion of their husbands. This opens the door for their discipleship.

Single students who reside in dorms may have an easy time finding a meeting place for Bible studies. Other single women may be able to meet in an open park or a restaurant, depending on the freedom women are allowed in their society.

Jansen has commented that we need to think of the title "pastor" as a verb rather than as a noun or title. "It is something we do. We do not need the title. There are many spiritual gifts. Create an environment in which everyone can use her spiritual gift. We do this first by modeling as a team and teaching specifically on spiritual gifts. We are trying to stay away from a one person show" (Jansen 2000:193).

Using all available resources in the discipleship process is extremely important. If there is a gifted leader in the group, all too often the ministry focuses on this person. Solid teaching on spiritual gifts, followed by the appointment of qualified individuals for specific ministries can give great impetus to the maturation of a fellowship of believers.

Successful Models

A women's fellowship in the Middle East provides a successful model for discipleship. Present in the believers meeting are two missionary women and six believers with an

Arab Muslim background. The women are each less than nine months old in the Lord. Several are working as house helpers for the missionaries. Tea and cookies are served during a fellowship time prior to the teaching. All then go to the prayer room. Shoes are removed and scarves placed on heads. The women stand shoulder to shoulder with uplifted hands. The leader calls out in Arabic, "God is Great. I testify that there is no God but God, and Isa is the word of God." Following this, the women are seated on carpets and give testimonies of how the Lord is working in their lives. They also begin to pray for personal needs, which include the salvation of spouses, needs for jobs, or healings for friends. After spontaneous intercession, the group recites the Lord's Prayer together.

The meeting continues with singing worship choruses in Arabic tunes. All then commence to chant verses from the Bible. Since most of the women are illiterate, this is an excellent way to facilitate the memorization of God's word. It is a ritual common to all Muslims.

Next, Bible teaching is shared with the goal of trying to make it both spiritually and culturally relevant. Local illustrations are utilized. It is helpful that the culture of Jesus' day and that of the women have many similarities. Finally, the women recite the ceremonial words of I Corinthians 11 together as they break bread and share the Lord's Supper (R. Love 2000:185–186).

This is an excellent example of a contextualized worship service for women coming out of Islam. It incorporates a number of elements appreciated by Middle Eastern women, such as meeting with women only; emphasizing food and fellowship; removing shoes and wearing head coverings; interceding for felt needs; and contextualizing the style of prayer, biblical teaching, chants, memorization, and the Lord's Supper. All of this is carried out at a level appropriate for the participants.

A teaching method that has been used successfully among Muslim women is the chronological style of telling biblical stories. Author A.H. writes about this.

"Chronological Bible storying is a win/win approach because it waits until the individual has all the information before asking for a decision. It is biblically sound in that it presents the theological base for the need for a savior before presenting Jesus as the savior. For example, Paul and Stephen presented a chronological overview of the Old Testament in their witness encounters. Jesus himself, as he walked with two disciples on the Emmaus road after his resurrection, started his encounter with the books of Moses and the prophets before he talked about himself as the Messiah. In addition, the process allows God to reveal himself and then Jesus to reveal himself before confronting the hard issue of Jesus' death and resurrection. After all the information has been presented, the person is asked to make a decision. For these reasons, I have found this method ideal for use with Muslim women.

"In addition, it allows me to teach the Bible to women in groups. By telling the story and talking about what the story teaches us about God, I'm not asking them to believe. I don't get into debates about which story (Quranic or biblical version) is true. I present the truth, help them discover the meaning for their lives during the dialogue time and leave the work of the Holy Spirit to the Holy Spirit (Acts 16:14)" (A. H. 2000:155).

While not denying any of the above, I have noticed that some Muslims get restless and even bored if the lessons go on and on. It will be up to the teacher to make the presentation in a gripping manner. Also, one needs to make a careful selection of material based on the audience's background and interest.

At times, there may be divine intervention in the discipleship process.

"'I prayed to receive Christ because my husband told me to,' this elegant, college-educated woman replied. Then she added, 'But after that, I decided I should study what we had gotten ourselves into. So I began to read the Bible seriously. Actually, I had read part of it back in Turkey in an English literature class. Now I began to study the Bible. I had the time. I wasn't enrolled in classes. So for several hours every day, I read the Bible and meditated on it.'...

"'One night I had a dream,' Suna remembered. 'I was in a fast-flowing sewer. I scrambled to get out. But the more I clawed for a handhold, the more I was sucked down. Suddenly a great strong hand came out of nowhere and lifted me up, and set me on solid ground. I stood in front of a glorious high throne. The Lord Jesus sat on the throne.'

"'I've taken you out of a filthy place. What are you going to do now?' the Lord Jesus said to Suna.

"'I'm going to read the Bible, and teach the Bible,' Suna answered" (Adeney 2000:108).

Once again a dream takes center stage in the Lord's dealing with a Muslim woman. Suna was drawn to teach the Bible through a dramatic encounter with Christ.

Cultural Differences in Morality

Ethics and morality are often defined by cultural norms. There will be times when common and acceptable behavior for a Muslim woman will be in direct opposition to biblical teaching. I think of lying as a prime example. As I talk with missionaries from many different Islamic countries, I find that a common frustration is with the way Muslims emotionally and cognitively deal with what constitutes a lie. After a great deal of research, I conclude that most Muslims see nothing wrong with a blatant falsehood, as long as the result is not harmful to anyone. If it crosses an ethereal line so that it causes pain or hurt, then it is perceived as a sin.

Another moral dilemma is presented when a Muslim woman is caught stealing. She says, "You make such a lot of fuss about nothing at all. We do not call stealing what you call stealing. If you do not want things taken, lock them up. That is our custom. Anything left lying about is always recognized among us as belonging to the first person who finds it. We do not steal money or big things; after all, what are eggs? I was taught to steal eggs and poultry by my father when I was a little girl, and I am an expert the same as he is" (Fisk 1951:141).

In a recent visit to Nouakchott, Mauritania, I was told to be sure to lock the guest-room door when I went out to the verandah and down to the nearby bathroom. Otherwise the next-door neighbors would see the open room, cross the low wall, enter, and take anything they wanted from my possessions. So although Mrs. Fisk's experience pre-dated 1951, it is still very contemporary.

In light of these realities, there must be a strong emphasis on teaching and modeling biblical ethics. Muslim converts need to see and hear good examples of behavioral guidelines. It will take much repetition and patience to finally break sub-biblical cultural norms that have been deeply ingrained for generations.

Other discipleship tools that can be utilized include correspondence courses, biblical teaching on cassettes,

Christian radio programs, and writing letters of friendship. Each cultural setting will have its own opportunities and constraints. Creativity is called for. Sensitive experimentation will lead to styles of discipleship that can make a great impact.

Persecution

Sadly, there will be many instances where the new believer will experience deep emotional and even physical pain for her faith. In such times, how does the discipler relate to the suffering disciple? Linda Smith, in her testimony, says, "Though I will never suffer in the same way as a convert, as one who has come to live among them, I also encounter some suffering. I am sometimes misunderstood, rejected, mocked, looked down upon, ridiculed. I am a stranger in a sometimes very strange land. I have been threatened with deportation. I have been imprisoned. I am now a fingerprinted alien with all the possible repercussions that could bring.

"But what I have found essential is to 'walk my talk.' Over the years, I have discipled many women who are crushed, who have been abused, who have come out of awful home situations. As they become Christians, I talk with them about the biblical way to face suffering" (Smith 2000:133).

To "walk our talk" is not always easy as we witness to believers with a Muslim background. We have so much; they have so little. If we are a resident in a hostile environment, our passport usually guarantees a retreat to a safe haven in times of dire circumstances. What the new believer most desires is a model, a guide who has also passed through fire and floods and yet has been faithful to the faith.

Bilquis Sheikh walked through a deep valley of emotional suffering subsequent to her conversion.

"At 3:00 in the morning my white bedside phone did clamor. I reached toward the instrument, my heart pounding.

No one would call at this hour unless there had been a death in the family. I picked up the phone and at first heard only heavy breathing. Then three words were thrown at me like stones:

"'Infidel. Infidel. Infidel.'

"The phone went dead. I lay back on my bed. What was it? One of the fanatics my uncles constantly warned me about? What might they do?

"'Oh Lord, You know that I don't mind dying. But I'm an awful coward. I cannot stand pain.... Oh, I pray that I will be able to bear pain if it comes.' Tears filled my eyes.... 'Lord. I'm sorry. Just let me walk with You through whatever comes next.'

"What did come next was a threatening, anonymous letter.... Then there was another letter and shortly still another. They all contained warnings. I was a turncoat and I would be treated as such.

"Late one afternoon in the early summer of 1967, about six months after my conversion, I stood in my garden with the crumpled remains of one such letter in my fist. It was particularly vitriolic, calling me worse than an infidel, a seducer of the faithful. True believers, the letter said, had to burn me out like gangrene is burned out of a healthy limb" (Sheikh 1978:96–97).

How threatening to be awakened at three in the morning and hear that word "infidel" repeated three times into one's ear. Many new converts would have been tempted to deny the Lord under such intense pressure, but not Bilquis. Such threats only seemed to strengthen her resolve to maintain her fidelity to the faith.

Subai is another example of such dedication.

"One day, called out of the house by the shouts of a group of male relatives, Subai was pushed to the center of the group. Her uncle screamed, 'Repent. Repent. Deny the Son of God!' "'No, He died for me and I have forgiveness of sins through His blood. He has given me everlasting life,' she bravely replied, trusting God to mask the tremble in her voice and glad for the baggy clothes that hid her shaking knees....

"This uncle brought about a lot of social pressure to the place where her father's home is located...Subai is not allowed to eat with her parents or siblings or wash clothes or drink from the common hand pump. One night as she laid down her bed roll on the ground to sleep, she found a snake inside, placed deliberately by this enemy. Another time her father, who usually defends her, was going to teach her a lesson. 'Get me milk and boil it immediately!' he ordered. Surprised and yet pleased that he would again drink from her hand, she quickly purchased the milk and boiled it up to pasteurize it. Feeling cold milk would be more refreshing, she purchased ice with her own money and quickly cooled down the hot pan in a pail. Transferring the cooled milk to another pan, balancing a glass with ice, she approached her father. He rose suddenly grasping his rubber shoe and brought it up forcefully under the pan, liberally splashing milk over her clothes, her hair and face. How surprised he was that she was not scalded! A soft answer turns away wrath. Deeds of kindness, like cooling the milk, always profit the doer" (Ilaim n.d.:39).

How many mature Western Christians could endure such pressure to deny Jesus? Few have been tested to this extent.

Male converts frequently have the option of flight. This is especially true in the Middle East. Hundreds, if not thousands of persecuted converts have fled to a European country where they could start their life over. Such a choice is seldom possible for the female believer.

Faduma professed faith in Christ. Upon hearing of this "traitorous act," her family was devastated. Her mother cried for three days. Rumors spread that Faduma had cut her hair, was wearing a mini-skirt, and was about to marry a "dog." Wisely, this new convert returned to her home and dispelled the negative cultural rumors. The offense of the Cross had to remain but, as far as possible, other alienating factors were avoided.

In 1896, Lilias Trotter, a long-term missionary in North Africa, took a strong stand on the importance of new believers refusing to observe the Ramadan fast.

"The breaking of the Ramadan fast, in particular, provided the acid annual test for any convert. This being the ideal, courageous stand, Lilias took every measure possible to strengthen the believers toward that end, having special 'coffee drinkings' during the day at their home and then evening Magic Lantern meetings (the precursor to slide shows) for the encouragement of their faith. Yet it was with 'pain and perplexity' that she considered the enormous, almost unbearable, cost to the one who chose to take this stand; it might mean loss of jobs and status for the men, loss of husbands and honor for the women. Perhaps even more disturbingly, the act of breaking the fast by the young implied a dishonoring of their elders.

"Taitum, who broke the fast secretly, articulated to Lily the plight of the women: 'No one can know what it is for a woman to break Ramadan. No one will let a room to her, or buy from her or sell to her—she is hooted like a carnival if she shows herself out in the street or even on her roof: she is looked on as an outcast woman—just that.' Knowing the grave consequences young men and women faced, when they weakened in their stance, Lilias comforted herself with the conviction that God understood: 'He is so gentle and patient with them, the blessed Spirit of God'" (Rockness 1999:136).

While I greatly admire the life and ministry of Ms. Trotter, I would have to disagree with her views on the Ramadan fast. As I write, Muslims worldwide are faithfully keeping this religious ritual. The Muslim girls in our dorm here in Manila are arising at three in the morning to cook, eat, and pray.

This is not an easy obligation to fulfill. I personally have scrupulously kept the demands of the fast on three occasions. My considered opinion is that this fast is optional for Christians. However, it is essential to emphasize that such abstinence from food and water during daylight hours for thirty days is not a legalistic, meritorious act. Rather it is a time to seek God and grow in grace.

If a female convert breaks the Ramadan fast, it is an act pregnant with serious consequences. She is considered a social and religious outcast. Is this the message of alienation that one wants to communicate? Unfortunately the view that it is necessary for converts to break the Ramadan fast has been passed on in North Africa by various missions and nationals. Only in recent years has there been some re-evaluation of these prohibitions.

Discipling women with Muslim backgrounds is a challenging and awesome task, but it is imperative. Walking away from a newly born-again convert is analogous to a mother discarding her newborn child. Without food (the Word), clothes (the covering of the Spirit), and loving embraces (the care of the community), a spiritual child, like a physical child, will slowly wither and die.

16

The Path Ahead

Nameless, anonymous, and scorned by a world that measures success by beauty, brains and brawn. Let's call her Ayesha, probably the world's most utilized female name.

It was a pleasantly cool afternoon. Gerry Aquino, my colleague in ministry, was sitting with me behind our tables of literature on the sidewalk in front of our Reading Center. He was talking patiently and graciously to the money-demanding Abdul, a Muslim extortionist who had harassed us for the past fifteen months.

Since I am the real focus of Abdul's demands, I was reading and generally trying to ignore our unwelcome daily guest. A few feet away, the JESUS film was on, attempting to penetrate and dispel the spiritual darkness of the small crowd of Muslims who were absorbing a message that could cost them everything but also give them wealth beyond measure.

She was perhaps six years old and dressed somewhat shabbily. Her young mother wore the ubiquitous and required *hijab* (veil), identifying her as a daughter of Ishmael. Ayesha's face was a study in character, history, pain, and fear. There was such a pensive depth in the slight, soft brown wrinkle across her forehead. Eyes flashed about registering apprehension. Somehow her face immediately assaulted my senses.

Slowly, my eyes dropped down over her slight body. Her clothes were ragged and soiled. I was then shocked by what I saw next. Ayesha's legs were deformed, spindly, and at the wrong angles. But the feet—there were no feet! Only stumps. No shoes. Only taut, callused flesh covering leg bones.

Mesmerized, I watched little Ayesha go into the Center with her mom. They sat on the stools and began to watch this Isa (Jesus) on the screen as he healed the demonic and made the blind man to see. I wondered what flitted through the mind of this precious child.

Three times she came out. She hobbled down the sidewalk, opened a garbage bag, and deposited her orange peelings. Shyly, she glanced at me with a mixture of bewilderment and fear in her eyes. I tried to talk with her, giving her my best warm, American smile. She was totally unsure of my persona and intent.

Finally the film was over. I cautiously approached little Ayesha and asked, "How are you?" in Tagalog. She leaped away from me and grabbed for the security of her mother's skirt. Refuge, safety, and insulation from all harm. Mom patted her shoulders in an automatic and oft-rehearsed gesture of assurance that conveyed warmth and unconditional love.

Soon, they walked away. I can still see in my mind's eye the bare flesh rhythmically, but not in good sync, pounding down on the harsh pavement. What does the future hold for this precious Muslim child who was created in the image of God? What jarring, spiteful words will she have to endure from her peers? Who will want to enter into a marital relationship with a cripple? Does little Ayesha have a future in her Islamic world?

And not only deformed Ayesha but also Muslim girls and women in general. Is there hope for social change? Hope for full acceptance as members of the human race? Hope for the freedom to become a Christian? Is there hope?

It's hard not to be seized with melancholy as I ponder these questions. Empirically, the evidence as documented in this book offers little hope for the average Muslim woman. But God does!

We rest our case with the sovereign Lord of the past, present, and future. Faith pushes the borders. It prays, it believes, it perseveres. As we seek to navigate through the fog, may we be committed to two responses: (1) On the macro level, let us continue to tenaciously pray for Muslim women worldwide; and (2) on the micro level, may we probe for the ways and means to be involved with our near neighbor in a sensitive, loving witness of salvation in Christ alone.

Hope—the very essence of our Christian faith.

Bibliography

A. H. "Discipleship of Muslim Background Believers
Through Chronological Bible Storying." In Love,
Fran and Jeleta Eckheart, eds., *Ministry to Muslim
Women: Longing To Call Them Sisters.* Pasadena,
Ca.: William Carey Library, 2000, pp. 146–173.

A. H. and M. B. "Refugees Evangelizing Muslims." In
Urban Mission, March 1998, pp. 31–36.

Abdul-Rauf, Muhammad. *The Islamic View of Women and
the Family.* New York: Robert Speller and Sons,
1977.

Abu-Nasr. "Death For Dishonor: Women Slain for
Perceived Wrongs." In *Press Enterprise,* Riverside,
Ca.: July 9, 2000, p. A-24.

Accad, Fouad Elias. *Building Bridges.* Colorado Springs,
Co.: Navpress, 1997.

Adeney, Miriam. *Daughters of Islam. Building Bridges
with Muslim Women.* Downers Grove, Il,
InterVarsity Press, 2000.

Afroz, Sultana. "Gender Issue and Gender Sensitivity in Program Management," an unpublished paper. Dhaka, Bangladesh: 1999.

Afza, Nazhat. "Woman in Islam." In Khurshid Ahmad, ed., *The Position of Woman in Islam*. Safat, Kuwait: Islamic Book Publishers, 1982 (3rd ed., 1993), pp. 3–26.

Ahmad, Khurshid. "The Tragedy of Woman in the West." In Khurshid Ahmad, ed., *The Position of Woman in Islam*. Safat, Kuwait: Islamic Book Publishers, 1982 (3rd ed., 1993), pp. 27–37.

Ahmed, Leila. *Women and Gender in Islam*. New Haven, Ct.: Yale University Press, 1992.

Al-Nahdah Magazine. Malaysia, 1996, p. 69.

Ali, Miriam with Jana Wain. *Without Mercy: A Mother's Struggle Against Modern Slavery*. London: Warner Books, 1995.

Al Munajjed, Mona. *Women in Saudi Arabia Today*. New York: St. Martin's Press, 1997.

Anway, Carol L. *Daughters of Another Path*. Lee's Summit, Mo.: Yawna Publications, 1996.

Attir, Mustafa O. "Ideology, Value Changes, and Women's Social Position in Libyan Society." In Fernea, Elizabeth Warnock, ed., *Women and the Family in the Middle East*. Austin, Tx.: University of Texas Press, 1985, pp. 121–133.

Badawi, J. A. *The Status of Woman in Islam*. UK: Islamic Propagation Centre International, n.d.

Badawi, Jamal A. *The Muslim Woman's Dress*. Plainfield, In.: Muslim Students' Association, 1980.

_____. *Polygamy in Islamic Law*. Plainfield, In.: American Trust Publication, n.d.

_____. *Gender Equity in Islam*. Plainfield, In.: American Trust Publication, 1995.

Badran, Margot. *Feminists, Islam, and Nation*. Princeton, NJ.: Princeton University Press, 1995.

Badran, Margot and Miriam Cooke, Eds. *Opening the Gates*. Bloomington, In.: Indiana University Press, 1990.

Barakat, Halim. "The Arab Family and the Challenge of Social Transformation." In Fernea, Elizabeth Warnock, ed., *Women and the Family in the Middle East*. Austin, Tx.: University of Texas Press, 1985, pp. 27–48.

Barnes, Virginia Lee and Janice Boddy. *Aman, The Story of a Somali Girl by Aman*. As told to Virginia Lee Barnes and Janice Boddy. London: Bloomsbury Publishing, 1994.

Bartlotti, Debi. "Muslim Women in Crisis." In Love, Fran and Jeleta Eckheart, eds. *Ministry to Muslim Women: Longing To Call Them Sisters*. Pasadena, Ca.: William Carey Library, 2000, pp. 21–32.

Beck, Lois and Nikki Keddie. *Women in the Muslim World*. Cambridge, Ma.: Harvard University Press, 1978.

Betteridge, Anne H. "To Veil or Not to Veil: A Matter of Protest or Policy." In Nashat, Guity ed., *Women and Revolution in Iran*. Boulder, Co.: Westview Press, 1983, pp. 109–128.

Brien, Nell. *A Veiled Journey*. Chatswood, NSW, Australia: Mira Books, 2000 (fiction).

Brooks, Geraldine. *Nine Parts of Desire*. New York: Doubleday, 1995.

Butcher, Muriel. *By Faith, Character Cameos from North Africa*. Upper Darby: North Africa Mission, n.d.

Callaway, Barbara and Lucy Creevey. *Islam, Women, Religion, and Politics in West Africa.* Boulder, Co.: Lynne Rienner Publishers, 1994.

Chaudhry, Hafeez-ur-Rehman. "Pirs, Shrines and Women." In Al Mushir, vol. 37/3, 1995, pp. 49–61.

Chaudhry, Muhammad Sharif. *Women's Rights in Islam.* Delhi: Adam Publishers and Distributors, 1991.

Colgate, Julia. *Invest Your Heart.* Unpublished paper.

Cosar, Fatma Mansur. "Women in Turkish Society." In Beck, Lois and Nikki Keddie, eds., *Women in the Muslim World.* Cambridge, Ma.: Harvard University Press, 1978, pp. 124–140.

Coulson, Noel and Doreen Hinchcliffe. "Women and Law Reform in Contemporary Islam," In Beck, Lois and Nikki Keddie, eds., *Women in the Muslim World.* Cambridge, Ma.: Harvard University Press, 1978, pp. 37–68.

Dagher, Hamdun. *The Position of Women in Islam,* trans. Villach, Austria: Light of Life, 1995.

Daniszewski, John. "Female Circumcision Ban Nullified." In *Los Angeles Times*, June 25, 1997.

Davis, Susan Schaefer. "Working Women in a Moroccan Village." In Beck, Lois and Nikki Keddie, eds., *Women in the Muslim World.* Cambridge, Ma.: Harvard University Press, 1978, pp. 416–433.

Dareer, Asma El. *Woman, Why Do You Weep?* London: Zed Press Ltd., 1983.

Deaver, Sherri. "The Contemporary Saudi Woman." In E. Bourguignon, ed., *A World of Women.* New York: Praeger, 1980.

de Souza, Alfred, ed. *Women in Contemporary India and South Asia.* New Delhi: Manohar Publications, 1980.

Dwyer, Daisy Hilse. "Women, Sufism, and Decision-Making." In Beck, Lois and Nikki Keddie, eds., *Women in the Muslim World*. Cambridge, Ma.: Harvard University Press, 1978, pp. 585–598.

Eickelman, Christine. *Women and Community in Oman*. New York: New York University Press, 1984.

Eile, Lena. *Jando—The Rite of Circumcision and Initiation in East African Islam*. Lund, Switzerland: Plus Ultra, 1990.

el-Badry, Sheik Yousef. Quoted in "Verbatim," *TIME*, November, 17, 1997, p. 9.

el-Messiri, Sawsan. "Traditional Urban Women in Cairo." In Beck, Lois and Nikki Keddie, eds., *Women in the Muslim World*. Cambridge, Ma.: Harvard University Press, 1978, pp. 522–540.

Faruqi, Lamya al. *Women, Muslim Society and Islam*. Plainfield, In.: American Trust Publications, 1988.

Ferdows, Adele K. and Amir H. Ferdows. "Women in the Shii Fiqh: Images Through the Hadith." In Nashat, Guity, ed., *Women and Revolution in Iran*. Boulder, Co.: Westview Press, 1983, pp. 55–68.

Fernea, Elizabeth Warnock. *Guests of the Sheik: An Ethnography of an Iraqi Village*. Garden City, NY: Doubleday, 1969.

_____. *A Street in Marrakech*. Garden City, NY: Doubleday, 1980.

_____. *In Search of Islamic Feminism*. New York: Anchor Books, 1998.

Fernea, Elizabeth Warnock, ed. *Women and the Family in the Middle East*. Austin, Tx.: University of Texas Press, 1985.

Fernea, Elizabeth Warnock and Basima Qattan Bezirgan. *Middle Eastern Muslim Women Speak.* Austin, Tx.: University of Texas Press, 1977.

Fernea, Elizabeth Warnock and Robert A. Fernea. *The Arab World.* Garden City, NY: Doubleday, 1987.

Fischer, Michael M. J. "On Changing the Concept and Position of Persian Women." In Beck, Lois and Nikki Keddie, eds., *Women in the Muslim World.* Cambridge, Ma.: Harvard University Press, 1978, pp. 189–215.

Fisk, Eric G. *The Prickly Pear.* Chicago: Moody Press, 1951.

Fluehr-Lobban, Carolyn. *Islamic Society in Practice.* Gainesville, Fl.: University Press of Florida, 1994.

Freed, Ralph. *Reach Arabs For Christ.* Chatham, NJ: Trans World Radio, 1972.

Garceau, Scott and Therese. "Women in Peril." Review in *The Philippine Star,* Manila, 2000, p. L-4.

Ghani, Mufti Muhammed Abdul. *Rights of Husband and Wife.* Trans. by Zameerul Hassan. Delhi: Dini Book Depot, (3rd ed.) 1981.

Glaser, Ida and Napoleon John. *Partners or Prisoners? Christians Thinking About Women and Islam.* Carlisle, Cumbria, UK: Solway, 1998.

Goodwin, Jan. *Price of Honor.* New York: Plume-Penguin Books, 1994.

Haddad, Yvonne. "Traditional Affirmations Concerning the Role of Women As Found in Contemporary Arab Islamic Literature." In Smith, Jane I., ed., *Women in Contemporary Muslim Societies.* Lewisburg, Pa.: Bucknell University Press, 1980, pp. 61–86.

_____. "The Role of Women in Islam." In *Living Among Muslims*. Edited by John Knox Center for International Reform: Geneva, 1987, pp. 44–60.

Haddad, Yvonne Yazbeck and Adair T. Lummis. *Islamic Values in the United States*. New York: Oxford University Press, 1987.

Haddad, Yvonne Yazbeck, ed. *The Muslims of America*. New York: Oxford University Press, 1991.

Haeri, Shahla. "Mutah." In *The Oxford Encyclopedia of the Modern Islamic World*. New York: Oxford University Press, 1995, pp. 212–213.

_____. "The Institution of Mut'a Marriage in Iran: A Formal and Historical Perspective." In Nashat, Guity, ed., *Women and Revolution in Iran*. Boulder, Co.: Westview Press, 1983, pp. 231–251.

Hermansen, Marcia K. "Two-Way Acculturation: Muslim Women in America Between Individual Choice and Community Affiliation." In Haddad, Yvonne Yazbeck, ed., *The Muslims of America*. New York: Oxford University Press, 1991, pp. 188–201.

Hijab, Nadia. *Womanpower—The Arab Debate on Women at Work*. Cambridge: University Press, 1988.

Hitching, Bob. *McDonalds, Minarets and Modernity*. Seven Oaks, Kent, England: Spear Publications, 1996.

Holliday, G. Y. "Work for Moslem Women in Persia." In *Methods of Mission Work Among Moslems*, papers read at the First Missionary Conference on behalf of the Mohammedan World, held at Cairo April 4–9, 1906. New York: Fleming H. Revell, 1906, pp. 111–115.

Hussain, Fida. *Wives of the Prophet*. Lahore, Sh. Muhammad: Ashraf, 1952 (5th ed., 1980).

Ilaim. *What Is That In Your Hand?* Christar. Unpublished manuscript, n.d.

Institute for the Study of Islam and Christianity. "Egypt: Islamist Victory on 'Female Circumcision.'" In ISIC Bulletin, London, August–September, 1997, p. 6.

Ismail, Iljas. *Islamic Ethics and Morality.* Manila: CONVISLAM, 1980.

Jones, V. R. and L. Bevan. *Women in Islam.* Lucknow, India: The Lucknow Publishing House, 1941.

Jung, Anees. *Night of the New Moon, Encounters with Muslim Women in India.* New Delhi: Penguin Books, 1993.

Juned, Pehin Haji Abdul Aziz. "Circumcision In Islam." In *Al-Nahdah,* Kuala Lumpur, Malaysia, December, 1996, pp. 9–10.

Kaith, Agnes Newton. *Children of Allah.* Boston: Little, Brown and Company, 1965.

Kerr, David A. "Mary, Mother of Jesus, in the Islamic Tradition: A Theme for Christian Muslim Dialogue." In *Encounter* (Documents for Muslim Christian Understanding). Rome: Pontificio Istituto di Studi Arabi e d'Islamistica, May, 1989, pp. 5–17.

Khan, Mazhar Ul Haq. *Purdah and Polygamy.* Peshawar: Nashiran-e-ilm-o-taraqiyet, 1972.

Khan, Muhammad Muhsin. *The Translation of the Meanings of Sahih.* Al-Bukhari, Arabic-English, Vols. 1-9. Beirut: Dar Al Arabia. n.d.

Khan, S. *Why Two Women Witnesses?* London: Ta Ha Publishers, 1993.

Khan, Wahiduddin. *Woman Between Islam and Western Society.* New Delhi: Al-Risala Books, 1995.

Khattab, Huda. *The Muslim Woman's Hand Book*. London: Ta-Ha Publishers, 1993.

Kunna, Ibrahim M., ed. *Miscellaneous Questions And Answers for the Muslim Women*. Riyadh: Darussalam, 1996

Laube, Lydia. *Behind the Veil: An Australian Nurse in Saudi Arabia*. Kent Town, South Australia: Wakefield Press, 1991.

Lemu, B. Aisha and Fatima Heeren. *Woman in Islam*. Leicester, England: The Islamic Foundation, 1978.

Love, Fran. "Church Planting that Includes Muslim Women." In *International Journal of Frontier Missions*, Vol. 13:3, July–Sept. 1996, pp. 135–138.

Love, Fran and Jeleta Eckheart, eds. *Ministry to Muslim Women: Longing To Call Them Sisters*. Pasadena, Ca.: William Carey Library, 2000.

Love, Rick. *Muslims, Magic, and the Kingdom of God*. Pasadena, Ca.: William Carey Library, 2000.

McGirk, Tim. In *Time*, April 21, 1997.

Mahdavi, Shireen. "The Position of Women in Shi'a Iran: Views of the Ulama." In Fernea, Elizabeth Warnock, ed., *Women and the Family in the Middle East*. Austin, Tx.: University of Texas Press, 1985, pp. 255–268.

Maher, Vanessa. *Women and Property in Morocco*. Cambridge: Cambridge University Press, 1974.

Mahmoody, Betty. *Not Without My Daughter*. New York: St. Martin's Press, 1987.

Mallouhi, Christine. *Mini-Skirts, Mothers and Muslims*. Kent, England, Spear, n.d.

Maudoodi, Abul A'la. *The Laws of Marriage and Divorce in Islam*. Safat, Kuwait: Islamic Book Publishers, 1983 (2nd ed., 1993).

Maududi, S. Abul A'la. *Purdah and the Status of Woman in Islam*. Lahore: Islamic Publications, 1993. (First published in 1972.).

Mernissi, Fatima. *Beyond the Veil*. Cambridge, Mass.: Schenkman Publishing Company, 1975.

_____. *Women and Islam*. Trans. by Mary Jo Lakeland. Oxford, UK: Blackwell, 1991.

_____. *The Forgotten Queen of Islam*. Trans. by Mary Jo Lakeland. Minneapolis, Mn.: University of Minnesota Press, 1993.

Mitton, Roger. "Islam Calling." In *Asiaweek*, Hong Kong, July 18, 1997.

Mosteshar, Cherry. *Unveiled: One Woman's Nightmare in Iran*. New York: St. Martin's, 1996.

Minces, Juliette. "Women in Algeria." Trans. by Nikki Keddie. In Beck, Lois and Nikki Keddie, eds., *Women in the Muslim World*. Cambridge, Ma.: Harvard University Press, 1978, pp. 159–171.

Mirza, Nathan. "An Analysis of the Cases of Five Muslims Who Became Christians." Thesis for BD degree at Near East School of Theology. Beirut, Lebanon, June 1970.

Moors, Annelies. *Women, Property and Islam*. New York: Cambridge University Press, 1995.

Muhsen, Zana with Andrew Crofts. *Sold. One Woman's True Account of Modern Slavery*. London: Warner Books, 1991.

Musk, Bill A. *The Unseen Face of Islam*. Eastbourne, England: MARC, 1989.

_____. *Touching the Soul of Islam*. Crowborough, England: MARC, 1995.

Nadvi, Mohammad Zafeeruddin. *Modesty and Chastity in Islam*, Trans. by Sharif Ahmed Khan. Safat, Kuwait: Islamic Book Publishers, 1982.

Nadwi, Syed Abul Hasan Ali. *Muslims in the West.* Leicester, England: The Islamic Foundation, 1983.

Naipaul, V. S. *Beyond Belief.* New York: Random House, 1998.

Nashat, Guity, ed. *Women and Revolution in Iran.* Boulder, Co.: Westview Press, 1983.

Nasr, Seyyed Hossein. *Ideals and Realities of Islam.* Boston: Beacon Press, 1966, 1972.

Nasrin, Taslima. *Shame: A Novel.* Prometheus Books, 1997.

Oram, Elizabeth. "Zainaba." In Badran, Margot and Miriam Cooke, eds., *Opening the Gates.* Bloomington. In.: Indiana University Press, 1990, pp. 63–71.

Pakizegi, Behnaz. "Legal and Social Positions of Iranian Women." In Beck, Lois and Nikki Keddie, eds., *Women in the Muslim World.* Cambridge, Ma.:, Harvard University Press, 1978, pp. 216–226.

Parshall, Phil. *Bridges to Islam.* Grand Rapids, Mi.: Baker Book House, 1983.

_____. *Beyond the Mosque.* Grand Rapids, Mi.: Baker Book House, 1985.

_____. *The Cross and the Crescent.* Waynesboro, Ga: Gabriel Publishing, 2002.

Peters, Emrys L. "Women in Four Middle East Communities." In Beck, Lois and Nikki Keddie, eds., *Women in the Muslim World.* Cambridge, Ma., Harvard University Press, 1978, pp. 311–350.

Pickthall, Muhammad Marmaduke. *The Cultural Side of Islam*. Delhi: Islamic Book Trust, 1927 (reprint) 1982.

Pillsbury, Barbara L. K. "Being Female in a Muslim Minority in China." In Beck, Lois and Nikki Keddie, eds. *Women in the Muslim World*. Cambridge, Ma.: Harvard University Press, 1978.

Qawl-ul-Haq Publications. *Women in Islam*. Qawl-ul-Haq Publications, 1991.

Rahman, Fazlur. *Major Themes of the Quran*. Minneapolis: Bibliotheca Islamica, 1994.

"Syariah Courts Must Be Fair to Women." In *Al-Nahdah*, December 1996, p.69. Regional Islamic Da'wah Council of Southeast Asia and the Pacific (RISEAP).

Rockness, Miriam Huffman. *A Passion for the Impossible: The Life of Lilias Trotter*. Wheaton, Il.: Harold Shaw Publishers, 1999.

Saadawi, Nawal El. *The Hidden Face of Eve*. Hetata, Dr. Sherif, trans., ed. London: Zed Press, 1980.

Saints Herald. Vol. 132:17, November 1985, pp. 18–24.

Sasson, Jean. *Princess*. New York: William Morrow and Company, 1992.

_____. *Princess Sultana's Daughters*. New York: Doubleday 1994.

_____. *Desert Royal*. London: Bantam Books, 1999.

Scattolin, Giuseppe. "Women in Islamic Mysticism." In *Encounter (Documents for Muslim-Christian Understanding)*. Rome: Pontificio Istituto di Studi Arabi e d'Islamistica, October 1993.

Schimmel, Annemarie. *Mystical Dimensions of Islam.* North Carolina: University of North Carolina Press, 1981.

_____. *My Soul Is a Woman.* New York: Continuum, 1997.

Shaaban, Bouthaina. *Both Right and Left Handed—Arab Women Talk About Their Lives.* Bloomington, In.: Indiana University Press, 1988.

Sheikh, Bilquis with Richard H. Schneider. *I Dared to Call Him Father.* Grand Rapids, Mi.: Chosen Books, 1978.

Shukri, Ahmed. *Muhammedan Law of Marriage and Divorce.* New York: AMS Press, 1966.

Siddiqi, M. I. *Rights of Allah and Human Rights.* Kazi Publications, 1981.

Smith, B. Linda. "The Sword of Christ: Muslim Women Make a Costly Commitment." In Love, Fran and Jeleta Eckheart, eds., *Ministry to Muslim Women: Longing To Call Them Sisters.* Pasadena, Ca.: William Carey Library, 2000, pp. 123–138.

Smith, Jane I., ed. *Women in Contemporary Muslim Societies.* Lewisburg, Pa.: Bucknell University Press, 1980.

Smith, Jane Idleman and Yvonne Yazbeck Haddad. *The Islamic Understanding of Death and Resurrection.* Albany, N.Y.: State University of New York Press, 1981.

Sonbol, Amira El Azhary, ed. *Women, the Family, and Divorce Laws in Islamic History.* Syracuse, NY: Syracuse University Press, 1996.

Stacey, Vivienne. *Women in Islam.* London: Interserve, 1995.

Stowasser, Barbara Freyer. *Women in the Quran, Traditions, and Interpretation.* New York: Oxford University Press, 1994.

Templeton, Charles. *Farewell To God.* Toronto: McClelland & Steward, Inc., 1996.

The Moslem World, 1929, p. 28. Quoted in Jones, V. R. and L. Bevan, *Women in Islam.* Lucknow, India: The Lucknow Publishing House, 1941, p. 127.

Thompson, A. Y. "Work Among Moslem Women in Cairo." In *Methods of Mission Work Among Moslems,* papers read at the First Missionary Conference on behalf of the Mohammedan World, held at Cairo April 4–9, 1906. New York: Fleming H. Revell, 1906, pp. 122–125.

Torrevillas, Domini M. "Parents' Woes." In "From the Stands," *Philippine Star,* February, 14, 1998.

Toubia, Nahid F. "The Social and Political Implications of Female Circumcision: The Case of the Sudan." In Fernea, Elizabeth Warnock, ed., *Women and the Family in the Middle East.* Austin: Tx.: University of Texas Press, 1985, pp. 148–159.

Van Sommer, Annie and Samuel M. Zwemer, eds. *Our Muslim Sisters.* New York: Fleming H. Revell, 1907 (2nd ed.).

Vieille, Paul. "Family Alliance and Sexual Politics." In Beck, Lois and Nikki Keddie, eds., *Women in the Muslim World.* Cambridge, Ma.: Harvard University Press, 1978, pp. 451–472.

Voorhees, Elizabeth C. Kay. *Is Love Lost? Mosaics in the life of Jane Doolittle "Angel Mother" in a Muslim Land.* Pasadena, Ca.: William Carey Library, 1988.

Waddy, Charis. *The Muslim Mind.* London: Longman, 1976, (2nd ed., 1982).

Walther, Wiebke. *Women In Islam.* Princeton, N.J.: Markus Wiener Publishers, 1995.

Warraq, Ibn. *Why I am Not a Muslim.* Amherst, N.Y.: Prometheus Books, 1995.

Waters, Kay. "Evangelism to and Through Family Networks." In Love, Fran and Jeleta Eckheart, eds., *Ministry to Muslim Women: Longing To Call Them Sisters.* Pasadena, Ca.: William Carey Library, 2000, pp. 174–190.

Wikan, Unni. *Behind the Veil in Arabia.* Chicago, Il: The University of Chicago Press, 1982.

Zuhur, Sherifa. *Revealing Reveiling.* Albany: University of New York, 1992.

Zwemer, Samuel. *Childhood in the Moslem World.* New York: Fleming H. Revell, 1915.

Zwemer, Dr. and Mrs. Samuel M. *Moslem Women.* Cambridge, Ma: The Central Committee on the United Study of Foreign Missions, 1926.

Other books available from
Authentic Media . . .

**Authentic
MEDIA**

129 Mobilization Dr
Waynesboro, GA 30830

706-554-1594
1-8MORE-BOOKS
authenticusa@stl.org

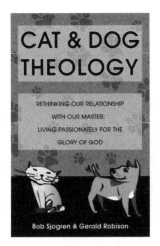

Cat and Dog Theology
Rethinking Our Relationship With Our Master

Bob Sjogren & Dr. Gerald Robison

"There is a joke about cats and dogs that conveys their differences perfectly. A dog says, 'You pet me, you feed me, you shelter me, you love me, you must be God.' A cat says, 'You pet me, you feed me, you shelter me, you love me, I must be God.' "

These God-given traits of cats ("You exist to serve me") and dogs ("I exist to serve you") are often similar to the theological attitudes we have in our view of God and our relationship to Him. Using the differences between cats and dogs in a light-handed manner, the authors compel us to challenge our thinking in deep and profound ways. As you are drawn toward God and the desire to reflect His glory in your life, you will worship, view missions, and pray in a whole new way. This life-changing book will give you a new perspective and vision for God as you delight in the God who delights in you.

1884543170   206 Pages

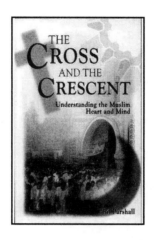

The Cross & the Crescent
Understanding the Muslim Heart and Mind

Dr. Phil Parshall

In this warm and personal book, the author looks at what Muslims believe and how this affects - and often doesn't affect - their behavior. Phil Parshall compares and contrasts Muslim and Christian views on the nature of God, sacred scriptures, worship, sin, and holiness.

Phil Parshall has served among Muslims since 1962 with International Christian Fellowshiop (now SIM) in Bangladesh and the Philippines. As a well-respected authority on Muslims, Dr. Parshall has taught courses on Islam at colleges and seminaries, and taught field seminars worldwide. He now resides in the Philippines with his wife, Julie where they minister among 30,000 Muslims in a Manila slum.

1884543685   320 Pages

A Guide to Short Term Missions
A Comprehensive Manual for Planning an Effective
Mission Trip

Dr. Leon Greene

Dr. Greene gives us a thorough look at the challenges and blessings facing anyone preparing for a short-term missions trip. He uses his experiences from over 30 short term missions trips to provide the reader with a one-stop guide to make the most of this opportunity. Includes:

- Timeline
- Passport
- How to Prepare
- Forming the Team
- Heath

- Immunizations
- Packing Checklist
- Emergency Plans & Disaster Relief
- Websites
- Other helpful resources

Dr. Leon Greene received his medical degree in 1969 at the Johns Hopkins University School of Medicine in Baltimore, Maryland. He has extensive experience in short-term missions and has participated in 20 medical and disaster relief missions since 1987. His mission work as included service in the Philippines, Mexico, Guatemala, Honduras, India, North Korea, and Rwanda. His first occupational love and passion are to reach the poor and needy with the love of Christ through medical care.

1884543731   336 Pages

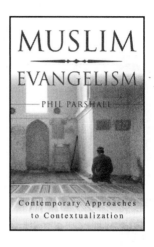

Muslim Evangelism
Contemporary Approaches To Contextualization
Revised Version of *New Paths In Muslim Evangelism*

Phil Parshall

It was this book which gave new, biblical meaning to the word "contextualization" and made that word the "hot topic" that it is in Muslim ministry today. If you want to understand deeply the issues at stake in Christian ministry among Muslims, then you must read this book.

Much has happened in our chaotic world since *New Paths In Muslim Evangelism* was first published in 1981. Muslims of the ultra-fundamentalist variety have terrorized millions. Westerners are perplexed. Are these "Followers of Muhammad" people of peace or are they religious fanatics bent on world domination?

In this important book, Phil Parshall seeks to acquaint the reader with the Muslim, not as a terrorist, but as one of the 1.3 billion who regard Islam as a "way of life" whose main concern is to provide for their families and to live in peace.

1-884543-79-0   304 Pages